YOUNG ADULTS DESE

YOUNG ADULTS DESERVE THE BEST

YALSA's COMPETENCIES IN ACTION

....

SARAH FLOWERS

for the Young Adult Library Services Association

AMERICAN LIBRARY ASSOCIATION

CHICAGO   2011

Sarah Flowers is the author of four nonfiction books for young people, including *The Reformation* (Lucent, 1995) and *The Age of Exploration* (Lucent, 1998). She wrote the chapter "Teens and Big Screen: Building a Video Collection to Bring Them Together," for *Thinking Outside the Book: Alternatives for Today's Teen Library Collections,* edited by C. Allen Nichols (Libraries Unlimited, 2004). She has written articles and reviews for *Voice of Youth Advocates, Young Adult Library Services,* and *School Library Journal,* and is currently the editor of *Young Adult Library Services.* She has worked as a young adult librarian, a supervisor of adult and young adult services, the manager of a community library, and as the deputy county librarian for the Santa Clara County Library in California. She was a member of the top forty distinguished alumni of the San Jose State School of Library and Information Science, and was a member of the first class (2002) of *Library Journal*'s "Movers and Shakers." She has been active in ALA and YALSA for many years, and served on YALSA's board of directors. She is currently YALSA's president-elect, and will serve as president for the 2011–2012 term.

© 2011 by the American Library Association. Any claim of copyright is subject to applicable limitations and exceptions, such as rights of fair use and library copying pursuant to Sections 107 and 108 of the U.S. Copyright Act. No copyright is claimed in content that is in the public domain, such as works of the U.S. government.

ISBN: 978-0-8389-3587-3

Printed in the United States of America
15 14 13 12 11   5 4 3 2 1

While extensive effort has gone into ensuring the reliability of information appearing in this book, the publisher makes no warranty, express or implied, on the accuracy or reliability of the information, and does not assume and hereby disclaims any liability to any person for any loss or damage caused by errors or omissions in this publication.

Library of Congress Cataloging-in-Publication Data
Flowers, Sarah, 1952-
  Young adults deserve the best: YALSA's competencies in action / Sarah Flowers for the Young Adult Library Services Association.
     p. cm.
  Includes bibliographical references and index.
  ISBN 978-0-8389-3587-3 (alk. paper)
  1. Young adult services librarians--United States. 2. Young adults' libraries--United States. 3. Libraries and teenagers--United States. 4. Core competencies. I. Young Adult Library Services Association. II. Title.
  Z682.4.Y68F58 2011
  027.62'6--dc22
                                                                          2010014148

Book design in Charis SIL and Soho Gothic Pro by Casey Bayer.

♾ This paper meets the requirements of ANSI/NISO Z39.48-1992 (Permanence of Paper).

ALA Editions also publishes its books in a variety of electronic formats.
For more information, visit the ALA Store at www.alastore.ala.org and select eEditions.

CONTENTS

APPENDIXES

INTRODUCTION

THIS BOOK is a companion to *Young Adults Deserve the Best: Competencies for Librarians Serving Youth* (2010), published by the Young Adult Library Services Association (YALSA), a division of the American Library Association. YALSA's core purpose, as articulated in its strategic plan, is "to advocate for excellence in library services to the teen population," and its "Big Audacious Goal" is "to be the driving force behind providing excellent library services to all teens." The competencies available at www.ala.org/yalsa/competencies are a big part of YALSA's mission to serve teens in libraries. They outline the skills, the knowledge, and the philosophy that should be a part of the makeup of every librarian who serves teens.

The competencies were developed in 1981, revised in 1998, revised again in 2003 to include principles of positive youth development, and revised and updated in 2010. Directors and trainers use them as a basis for staff development opportunities. They can also be used by school administrators and human resources directors to create evaluation instruments, determine staffing needs, and develop job descriptions.

This book, however, was written with the frontline young adult librarian in mind. Having a list of competencies is useful, but it is not enough. This book was written to show the librarian how to use the competencies to improve service to teens, to make teen services an integral part of the library and the community, and to grow professionally. It is not expected that the entry-level YA librarian will have all of the competencies to begin with. That's why they exist—to give the professional something to aim for and grow into.

This book is not intended to be the definitive book on young adult services. In fact, I will refer to many other books and resources that will be valuable to the young adult librarian. What I do hope to do is to give the librarian a place to start in thinking about where his or her job fits into the bigger picture of both the parent institution and young adult library services in general. I hope to show how the skills and knowledges listed in the competencies apply to real-life situations, and how you can start from them to make yourself the best young adult librarian you can be.

Many people, including many who work in libraries, find teenagers difficult to deal with. The young adult librarian may often be the only person in the library who is willing to stand up for teens and their service needs. By embracing that role, you have the opportunity to grow professionally and to bring value to your library, your community, and the library profession as a whole.

Throughout the book, the terms *teen* and *young adult* (or YA) are used interchangeably, and refer to young people in the age range of twelve to eighteen years, the definition that YALSA uses for young adult.

The first seven chapters each focus on one of the competency areas. I begin by citing the competencies, and then elaborate on them, offering examples of how to achieve the different points. Much of the book consists of suggestions for actions you can take to move toward achieving the competencies. Text boxes in each chapter have been contributed by my colleagues in young adult services, giving examples of how they have used the competencies in real-life situations. A list of further reading concludes each chapter. Chapter 8 discusses using the competencies to make the case for establishing a teen services department.

YALSA has been an inspiration to me for my whole library career. My YALSA colleagues are among the best and the brightest library professionals anywhere. I would like to give special thanks to those who contributed stories and examples for this book: Amy Alessio, Marc Aronson, Linda W. Braun, Nick Buron, Kelly Czarnecki, Lindsey Dunn, Francisca Goldsmith, Michele Gorman, Jodi Mitchell, Charli Osborne, Sara Ryan, Stephanie Squicciarini, and Diane P. Tuccillo. Finally, I would like to give special thanks and acknowledgment to my son, Mark Flowers, a YA librarian at Solano County Library in California. Not only did he contribute a story for this book, but talking with him about his experiences as a first-year professional gave me ideas for this book, and keeping him in mind as I wrote helped to steer me in the right direction.

chapter ONE

COMPETENCY AREA I
Leadership and Professionalism

THE LIBRARIAN will be able to:

1. Develop and demonstrate leadership skills in identifying the unique needs of young adults and advocating for service excellence, including equitable funding and staffing levels relative to those provided for adults and children.

2. Develop and demonstrate a commitment to professionalism and ethical behavior.

3. Plan for personal and professional growth and career development.

4. Encourage young adults to become lifelong library users by helping them to discover what libraries offer, how to use library resources, and how libraries can assist them in actualizing their overall growth and development.

5. Develop and supervise formal youth participation, such as teen advisory groups, recruitment of teen volunteers, and opportunities for employment.

6. Model commitment to building assets in youth in order to develop healthy, successful young adults.

7. Implement mentoring methods to attract, develop, and train staff working with young adults.

Why do the competencies begin with leadership and professionalism? Because leadership and professionalism are the keys to providing the best possible service to teens. The young adult librarian is often the only one in the library who really cares about young adults. The best way to start advocating for service excellence is to present yourself as a serious professional. Everything else follows from that.

Let's start with some statistics. In 2007, the Public Library Data Service (PLDS) survey included questions about young adult services in public libraries. This collaboration between the Public Library Association and the Young Adult Library Services Association (YALSA) represented the first time statistics have been collected on these services since the National Center for Educational Statistics published a survey on YA services in 1994. Out of 1,672 libraries that received the survey, 904 responded (a 54.1 percent response rate), and of those, 890 responded to the YA services questions (98.5 percent of responding libraries).[1]

Of the responding libraries, 772 (85 percent) indicated that they have a separate YA services department. Generally speaking, the larger the library or system, the more likely it was to have a separate YA services department. According to an analysis of the statistics done by Megan Mustafoff and Lauren Teffeau of the University of Illinois–Urbana Champaign, "About half (51.9 percent) of all libraries have at least one librarian FTE [full-time equivalent] dedicated to YA services. . . . Similarly, 62.2 percent of libraries have at least one YA staff person, either librarian or paraprofessional. In 1994, only 11 percent of libraries had a YA librarian."[2]

From all of the responding libraries, about 46 percent had a separate materials budget for young adult materials. This varied widely depending on library size, from 72 percent of the largest libraries having a separate budget line for YA materials to less than 1 percent of the smallest libraries. Larger libraries are also more likely to house YA materials in a separate area from adult and children's materials. Mustafoff and Teffeau found that

> In 1994, only 58 percent of libraries housed YA materials separately from other types of library materials. The 2007 PLDS survey indicates this number has risen to 83.9 percent of central or main libraries and 72.2 percent of branch libraries keeping YA materials in a separate area.[3]

These numbers are encouraging for YA librarians, but they are just the beginning.

Now go to local statistics. Your library keeps statistics. Find out what they are and how they are collected. Are circulation statistics kept for YA materials? If not, find out if they can be. Most integrated library systems (ILSs) generate circulation statistics, but you may have to dig into a big report to get to the level of finding out which YA materials circulate and how much. Create turnover reports (number of circulations/number of items) for each YA materials category. Look at a list of items that have holds (reserves) on them. Which YA items have the most holds? Which items have the highest ratio of holds to copies owned? These figures will help you in both developing your collection and demonstrating its value to your administration. You can also look at patron information. Again, you may have to dig down and do some of the math yourself to find out how many patrons ages twelve through eighteen your library has and how many items they have checked out, but it can often be done.

Next, look at statewide statistics. The states require annual reporting, and these numbers are collected either in a printed book or online. For example, California creates *California Library Statistics* each year. Every library in the state receives a copy of the printed book, and it is also available online at www.library.ca.gov/lds/librarystats.html.

Library Research Service of Colorado has a handy web page with links to public library statistics from all of the states that make them available online (www.lrs.org/public/other.php). Often these statewide statistics are not much help to the YA librarian, because the reports consider only system-level data. The reporting is for entire library systems, not individual branches, and while children's materials and programs are often listed as separate entries, YA are usually not. Still, the data can be of some use in getting an idea of how other libraries of your size are funded compared to your library, and how materials expenditures compare.

What does it all mean for you? Think of it this way: if there isn't a budget line for it, it doesn't really exist. So do some more research. Find out how your library is funded and how YA is funded. In many public libraries, young adult services is a subset of children's (or youth) services; in others, it is a part of adult services. In either case, start by finding out whether there is a separate line item in your library's materials budget for young adult materials. Is there a position that is specifically designated as a "young adult librarian" or "teen services librarian"? Are YA materials housed separately from children's and adult materials? The answers to these questions will give you an idea of where your library's administration stands on the issue of young adult services. But don't stop there. If YA positions and materials budget lines don't exist, it is possible to create them.

Start by reading YALSA's white paper, "The Benefits of Including Dedicated Young Adult Librarians on Staff in the Public Library," prepared by Don Latham and Audra Caplan (www.ala.org/ala/mgrps/divs/yalsa/profdev/ whitepapers/yastaff.cfm). The authors note that it is important to have young adult librarians on staff because "a significant percent of the American population is composed of adolescents and many of them are library users." Young adult librarians, they go on to note, "are age-level specialists who understand that teens have unique needs and have been trained especially to work with this particular population." These specialists understand that the "behavior, interests, and informational and social needs [of teens] are not the same as those of children or adults." Moreover, the library and the community as a whole are improved when the needs of teens are addressed. YA librarians can help other staff feel comfortable with teens and can provide teens with positive social interaction with adults, something that helps teens grow and helps them find their place in society.[4]

Now look over all the information you have collected and see what it says to you about how YA services could be improved in your library. If circulation of YA materials is 15 percent of the library's circulation but YA materials get only 2 percent of the materials budget, you can make a case that more money is needed in this area. If patrons ages twelve through eighteen are 30 percent of your library's user population, but are responsible for only 10 percent of circulation, you may need to look at how to build a collection or services that will be of greater appeal or use to teens. Statistics don't always tell the whole story, though. Talk to your local teens to find out how they are using (and not using) the library. We'll talk more about this in chapter 4.

A commitment to professionalism includes understanding what the profession of librarianship in general and young adult librarianship in particular expect of its practitioners. Start by reading (or rereading) the American Library Association (ALA) Bill of Rights. (See appendix A.) Consider which parts of this document are easy for you, and which are hard. Think about the hard things. Are they hard because your library doesn't support them? Are they hard because your personal background makes it difficult? Do a little research by reading the Interpretations of the Library Bill of Rights. (See appendixes.) These documents have been adopted by the ALA Council, and as such are policies of the American Library Association. They include background statements detailing the philosophy and history of the Bill of Rights, and may answer questions that you have about how to implement the Bill of Rights and how to respond to criticisms. Of particular interest for young adult librarians are the interpretations "Free Access to Libraries for Minors,"

In 1989, five librarians were hired by Berkeley (California) Public Library to provide a dedicated, but new, young adult service to the public. In 1990, we planned how to fulfill that assignment by formulating a team. Together we developed a management plan and approached the library's administration to request the formal reorganization that would provide the service with a "senior librarian" to serve as our point person (we worked in five different facilities) and as liaison to affiliate services such as collection development. Our plan was accepted and the library posted this position. Once that position was filled, we were able to make considerable headway because we had a voice at the collection budget table, with the school administration and school board, and even with the architects planning an expanded central library. Eventually, Teen Services became a formal personnel budget line as well.

Francisca Goldsmith
Library Staff Development Consultant and Editor
Berkeley, California

"Access for Children and Young Adults to Nonprint Materials," "Access to Resources and Services in the School Library Media Program," "Minors and Internet Interactivity," and "Labeling and Rating Systems."

Next, read ALA's Code of Ethics (appendix H) and consider how the values listed play out in your day-to-day work. Consider in particular item number one about equitable access and item number three about the user's right to privacy. Are these values expressed in your library's policies? Are teens specifically addressed in these policies? Is the privacy of teens respected to the same level that the privacy of adults is? Do teens have "equitable service policies; equitable access; and accurate, unbiased, and courteous responses to all requests"? If not, you can take leadership by proposing changes to the existing policies that will remedy these shortcomings. Often library administrations are not hostile to equitable access for teens; it just has never occurred to them that their policies may not express this in the best possible way.

Your own personal and professional growth and career development are your responsibility. Participating in professional associations and continuing education are two ways to do that. Professional associations can range from local support groups (e.g., Bay Area Young Adult Librarians), to state associations, to national associations like ALA and YALSA. Yes, it costs money to join these organizations, and in most cases it comes out of your own pocket, but think of it as a statement to yourself and your library administration that you consider yourself a professional. In most organizations, membership offers a journal (either online or paper), some kind of online information, and in some cases a membership directory for making contacts.

Joining these organizations creates a three-way benefit: membership helps you keep up to date in your profession, you can bring information back to your school or library, and you can benefit the professional organization by contributing your own experiences to keep it up to date. In order to stay current and relevant, for example, YALSA needs a continued infusion of new members who are actively working in the field of young adult services. An association that doesn't bring along new members is an obsolete association.

Besides the cost of membership, another obstacle to being active in a professional organization is the need to attend conferences. Many libraries have limited or no funds for travel, and this can make it difficult to be a committee member. However, YALSA and other organizations are beginning to offer many different ways of being involved. ALA has been working on plans for electronic member participation. YALSA has entire committees composed of "virtual members" who participate electronically but are not required to attend conferences. In addition, YALSA has a wiki with pages for creating booklists and other content. If you are a member of ALA, you are automatically a member of at least one community on ALA Connect, ALA's online community. ALA Connect is a web platform created to promote communication and collaboration among ALA members. Discussion boards, chat rooms, and the ability to create one's own community of like-minded library people are a few of the features it offers. YALSA is actively hosting

Planning for personal and professional growth started right away for me. During my first month of working in my current position, I received a call asking if I wanted to serve on the conference planning committee for the Youth Services Section of the New York Library Association. I said yes and was on the committee, serving as chair or co-chair, for six years, advocating for increased conference programs for teen services. Since then I also served as treasurer of YSS and was very active in YALSA (various committees, task forces, and now the board of directors). With each role I learned new things that have helped me serve "my" teens and all of our library patrons better.

Stephanie A. Squicciarini, MLS
Teen/Young Adult Services Librarian
Fairport (New York) Public Library

monthly online chats that are open to all members to discuss issues of interest, from cheap programming to advocacy and more. The chats are archived on the YALSA blog, so even if you can't participate live, you can still learn. Some conference programs, including YALSA's annual President's Program in 2010, are entirely virtual. You can look forward to more such opportunities in the future.

But still, face-to-face conferences can be extremely valuable for your professional growth, and many committee assignments are dependent upon your ability to attend conferences. So in preparing your request for conference attendance to your administration, consider the following:

- Examine the preliminary conference program and any other information available on the conference website. Make notes about which programs you plan to attend.
- Provide a short list of programs to your supervisor and/or colleagues and ask which ones they would like you to attend.
- Offer to prepare and deliver a short presentation for your colleagues upon your return from the conference. Provide copies of program handouts and share what you learned.
- Offer to blog about the conference so that your library can share what you are learning in real time.
- Be generous in offering to trade shifts with colleagues who will cover for you while you are gone.
- Demonstrate to your supervisor how you will pare expenses by, for example, sharing a hotel room or staying with a friend.
- Belong to the organization whose conference you wish to attend, and be prepared to sign up for "early bird" registration, both of which will save money.[5]

Your library may have a plan for your continuing education or it may not. Some states require a certain number of CE units each year, which can be obtained by taking classes in person or online or by attending conferences. But even if your library or your state does not have a plan, you can and should. You are a librarian—research your locality and find out what services and programs are offered nearby that can help you in your work. There are more and more online courses available as well, through YALSA and other organizations. Some of them are even free. Colleges and universities are putting content on YouTube, iTunes, and other online sites. The Infopeople Project in California (www.infopeople.org) offers both on-ground and online courses on library-related topics, and courses are now open to non–California residents. Infopeople also offers free webinars, webcasts, and podcasts, which are archived on the website. YALSA's blog is also a continuing source of information and education. Archived posts can be searched by topic or keyword. Podcasts on subjects of interest to YA librarians are posted there regularly and archived.

Once a year, sit down and create a continuing education plan for yourself. What are the topics you wish you knew more about? What can you do to increase your knowledge in these areas? It can be as simple as reading a new professional book. You can find reviews of these in any journal that serves librarians, including YALSA's journal, *Young Adult Library Services* (*YALS*). It may involve taking a course. Know what your library will pay for, how much time you can reasonably expect to take to attend courses, and how far in advance you need to ask. If you work in a union environment, read your contract. You may find that you can be reimbursed for at least some continuing education expenses, as long as they are approved by a supervisor. If this is not true for you, suggest it to your union steward as an item for the next round of negotiations. If you work for a large county or city library system, find out what kinds of courses are offered by their training department. These will probably be free, with supervisor approval. The courses will be unlikely to be directly related to libraries, but they may well include topics you can use on the job, such as how to make a presentation, how to handle difficult people, how to prepare yourself to be a supervisor, how to manage your time, and how to use specific types of software.

Make time in your workday or even your own time to read several professional journals. It is likely that you will be the only one in your library actively reading journals, such as *YALS,* that are specifically about young adult services. If you find an article that is particularly relevant to your library, share it with the rest of the staff. Don't inundate them with material or they will just toss without reading, but the occasional well-chosen article can help enlighten them as to what is going on in young adult services. Include your supervisor and your supervisor's supervisor in the distribution. They may be more focused on management issues than on what's going on in the trenches, and you can help keep them up to date and make them YA advocates.

Another good way to keep up on the profession is to follow library-related blogs. An RSS feed aggregator will help you keep up with who is posting new information. Try to step a little outside your own comfort area. If you are all about books, find a blog or two about technology. If you are a techie, be sure to keep up on books, too. Blogs will often point you to articles in journals and newspapers that are of value to you in your professional growth.

Subscribing to electronic discussion lists is another way to keep up on what is happening in the field. YALSA sponsors several of these. But if you do post to a list, be sure you do it in a professional manner. Most lists have "rules of conduct," but a lot of posting appropriately is just common sense. For example, one of the great benefits of electronic discussion lists is the ability to plug into the "collective brain" by asking for suggestions for book titles or programs.

How Can Youth Participation Be Accomplished in Your Library?

Youth participation in library decision-making requires that adults (librarians, administrators, members of the governing and advisory bodies) recognize that young adults can make a positive contribution, and that adults respect the rights of teens to participate in decisions on matters that affect them.

Projects involving youth should have the following characteristics:

- Be centered on issues of real interest and concern to youth
- Have the potential to benefit people other than those directly involved
- Allow for youth input from the planning stage forward
- Focus on some specific, doable tasks
- Receive adult support and guidance, but avoid adult domination
- Allow for learning and development of leadership and group work skills
- Contain opportunities for training and for discussion of progress made and problems encountered
- Give evidence of youth decisions being implemented
- Avoid exploitation of youth for work, which benefits the agency rather than the young adults
- Seek to recruit new participants on a regular basis
- Plan for staff time, funds, administrative support, transportation, etc., before launching the project
- Show promise of becoming an ongoing, long-term activity

From "YALSA Guidelines for Youth Participation in ALA/YALSA," prepared by the Youth Participation Committee and approved by the YALSA Board of Directors, July 1997. Revised June 2001 and March 2006.

But be sure to be professional about it, and don't waste the time of others or yourself. Be specific about what you are looking for, and tell your colleagues what you have already done so that they don't have to repeat your work.

Another way to be involved professionally that does not require travel is to write for professional journals. A good way to start is with reviews of young adult materials or professional materials. If you have never reviewed before, start by practicing on your own so you will have some sample reviews to submit with your application. *YALS* uses member reviews of professional materials. Other journals, including *Voice of Youth Advocates* (*VOYA*), *School Library Journal, Booklist,* and *ALAN Review* use reviewers who work directly with teens to review YA books and media as well as professional materials. Check their websites for application information and requirements, or watch the journals for notices about the need for reviewers in particular areas. You may also want to think about contributing articles to professional journals. *YALS* is entirely member-written. Each quarterly issue has a theme, and guidelines are available on YALSA's website. Contributing to these journals won't make you rich, but it will provide solid material for your résumé, which will help you demonstrate your commitment to the profession when you apply for jobs or promotions.

Another way to show your library's administration that you are a leader is to encourage young adults to become lifelong library users. Teens often think they know everything there is to know about the library, but of course we are adding new materials, formats, and services all the time. When you do class visits, tours, or even just chat with teens in the library, it is worthwhile to mention some of the library's resources that might be new to them. Keeping teens actively using the library helps them grow and learn, and as a bonus it helps to ensure that when they become tax-paying adults, they will continue to support the library.

As YALSA's youth participation guidelines state,

> Youth participation in library decision-making is important as a means of achieving more responsive and effective library and information service for this age group. It is even more important as an experience through which young adults can enhance their learning, personal development, and citizenship while making the transition into adulthood.[6]

There are many ways to involve teens in the library, from formal teen advisory groups and volunteer programs to less formal conversations with the teens who are in the library. In her book on library teen advisory groups, Diane P. Tuccillo says,

> We all want teens to become library users and supporters as they progress into adulthood. The best way to do that is to offer teens meaningful opportunities to become instrumental players in their libraries. . . . Ultimately, teen advisory boards lay a foundation for lifetime library use and support.[7]

An outstanding benefit of providing youth participation in libraries is the positive exposure it gives to library work as a possible future career. In the thirty-one years I have been working with teens in libraries, direct teen library contributions have always played a vital role. This involvement has included and continues to include assuring teen representation on adult library boards; offering high-functioning and well-respected library teen advisory groups; asking teens to directly plan and run programs and activities for peers; gathering input from teens about what they want to have in their teens spaces and collections; giving teens chances to attend special conferences and conduct author visits; and much more.

A payoff to making such teen library participation a priority is in watching some teens move forward into productive library careers themselves. I have witnessed a number of teens who have entered the school or public librarian fields, some of whom even have exciting teen services departments and teen advisory groups (TAGs) of their own. One library teen from long ago now has an extremely dynamic TAG at the Ketchikan Public Library in Alaska. Another brought a barely-there teen section at the Yuma Public Library in Arizona to life with a vibrant TAG presence. She left that job when she married and moved, but she brings the same knowledge and enthusiasm to her current school librarian position. A third formerly active teen library participant recently corresponded with me with questions about becoming a librarian, and since has made a decision to go to library school. These are just a few examples of how teen library participation can encourage and help to perpetuate our library profession and teen services library careers.

Diane P. Tuccillo
Teen Services Librarian
Poudre River Public Library District, Fort Collins, Colorado
Author, *Library Teen Advisory Groups* (Scarecrow Press, 2005) and *Teen-Centered Library Service: Putting Youth Participation into Practice* (Libraries Unlimited, 2010)

If your library does not have an existing teen advisory board or any formal type of youth participation, start by looking at YALSA's "Guidelines for Youth Participating in Libraries" and some of the resources listed at the end of this chapter. Think about what type of youth participation is your greatest need. Talk to the teens who currently visit the library about what kind of participation they would be interested in. Find out if your town has a youth advisory commission and go to them for input as well.

Teen advisory groups and teen volunteer programs not only give teens the recognition, empowerment, and support they need, they are vital to the health of the library and the community. Every part of teen services—collections, programs, facilities, services—can benefit from teen input. And teens benefit as well. Not only do these types of opportunities give teens valuable experience and validation, they introduce the rest of the library staff and members of the community to teens who are working positively to make the world a better place. Additionally, many teens have started as members of advisory boards or as library volunteers, and have gone on to work for the library, perhaps first as pages or clerks, and even eventually as a new generation of librarians.

Another way to show leadership in the profession is to mentor others in working with young adults. Involve local library staff in working with young adult programming. Staff at all levels can be encouraged to work actively and creatively with teens. Be aware of who the other young adult specialists are in your area. While you may be the only one at your library, there are others in

So many young adult librarians are the only one in their library, or one of just a few. It's crucial that we reach out to each other and help with suggestions. In Illinois very few libraries can afford to send staff to conferences that involve airplane travel and hotels. When I have met Illinois YA folks who can travel, I continually nominate them for things, check in on them at conferences, and help them get involved any way I can. I also know most of the YA folks at public libraries in the state, and several school folks, either virtually or through meeting at local events. We have to support the YA librarian community to keep it going. I enjoy getting calls and visits from staff at other libraries, too, and make a point to try and treat them to coffee or lunch. It doesn't take much effort or time to encourage other people.

Amy Alessio
Teen Coordinator
Schaumburg Township (Illinois) District Library

your county, metro area, or state. Make of point of getting together with them to share information and encouragement. There may be a local support group of YA librarians, but if there isn't, you can start one. Even getting together for drinks or coffee every few months can inspire all of you to greater heights. Think about what you can do to mentor and encourage others.

Leadership and professionalism are the basic building blocks for every successful librarian. Use these competencies to analyze your own level of professionalism and to start planning for your future as a leader in your library and in YA services.

SUGGESTED READING

Agosto, Denise. "Why Do Teens Use Libraries? Results of a Public Library Use Study." *Public Libraries* 46, no. 3:55–62.

Alessio, Amy, and Nick Buron. "Measuring the Impact of Dedicated Teen Service in the Public Library." *Young Adult Library Services* 4, no. 3:47–51.

Bernier, Anthony. "Young Adult Volunteering in Public Libraries: Managerial Implications." *Library Leadership and Management* 23, no. 3:133–39.

Edwards, Margaret A. *The Fair Garden and the Swarm of Beasts: The Library and the Young Adult,* centennial ed. Chicago: American Library Association, 2002.

Gillespie, Kellie M. *Teen Volunteer Services in Libraries.* Lanham, MD: Scarecrow Press, 2003.

Gorman, Michele, and Tricia Suellentrop. *Connecting Young Adults and Libraries: A How-to-Do-It Manual,* 4th ed. New York: Neal-Schuman Publishers, 2009.

Infopeople. http://infopeople.org.

King, Kevin A. R. "All I Really Need to Know about Teen Advisory Boards I Learned from . . ." *Voice of Youth Advocates* 28, no. 5:378–79.

Miller, Donna P. *Crash Course in Teen Services.* Westport, CT: Libraries Unlimited, 2008.

Suellentrop, Tricia. "Step Right Up: Teen Volunteers." *School Library Journal* 53, no. 12:24.

Tuccillo, Diane P. *Library Teen Advisory Groups.* Lanham, MD: Scarecrow Press, 2004.

Tuccillo, Diane P. "Successful Teen Advisory Groups." www.voya.com/2010/04/26/successful-teen-advisory-groups.

Tuccillo, Diane P. *Teen-Centered Library Service: Putting Youth Participation into Practice.* Westport, CT: Libraries Unlimited, 2010.

Walter, Virginia A., and Elaine Meyers. *Teens and Libraries: Getting It Right.* Chicago: American Library Association, 2003.

YALSA, with Audra Caplan. "The Benefits of Including Dedicated Young Adult Librarians on Staff in the Public Library: A White Paper." www.ala.org/ala/mgrps/divs/yalsa/profdev/whitepapers/yastaff.cfm.

YALSA, YALSA's Guidelines for Youth Participating in Libraries. www.ala.org/ala/mgrps/divs/yalsa/aboutyalsa/nationalyouth.cfm.

Younker, J. Marin. "Where Is the Love?" *School Library Journal* 52, no. 12:31.

Zilonis, Mary Frances, Carolyn Markuson, and Mary Beth Fincke. *Strategic Planning for School Library Media Centers.* Lanham, MD: Scarecrow Press, 2002.

NOTES

1. Public Library Association, *Public Library Data Service — Statistical Report 2007* (Chicago: PLA, 2007).
2. Megan Mustafoff and Lauren Teffeau, "Young Adult Services and Technology in Public Libraries: An Analysis of the 2007 Public Library Data Service." *Public Libraries* 47, no. 1:12.
3. Ibid., 13.
4. Don Latham and Audra Caplan, "The Benefits of Including Dedicated Young Adult Librarians on Staff in the Public Library: A White Paper." www.ala.org/ala/mgrps/divs/yalsa/profdev/whitepapers/yastaff.cfm.
5. Thanks to Kathleen Hughes on the PLA blog (http://plablog.org/2009/10/justifying-your-trip-to-pla-2010.html) for many of these ideas.
6. YALSA, "YALSA's Guidelines for Youth Participating in Libraries." www.ala.org/ala/mgrps/divs/yalsa/aboutyalsa/nationalyouth.cfm.
7. Diane P. Tuccillo, *Library Teen Advisory Groups* (Lanham, MD: Scarecrow Press, 2005), 1–2.

chapter TWO

COMPETENCY AREA II
Knowledge of Client Group

THE LIBRARIAN will be able to:

1. Become familiar with the developmental needs of young adults in order to provide the most appropriate resources and services.

2. Keep up to date with popular culture and technological advances that interest young adults.

3. Demonstrate an understanding of, and a respect for, diverse cultural, religious, and ethnic values.

4. Identify and meet the needs of patrons with special needs.

Knowledge of the client group is another area in which the young adult specialist may be the only person in the library who is taking responsibility. Many library staff members, not to mention other patrons, see teenagers as loud, unruly, difficult, and, frankly, scary. By being cognizant of the developmental needs of young adults, the youth specialist can not only provide appropriate services to the teens, but can help explain teens to the rest of the world. And you are the one who can remind everyone else that by creating a place where teens can belong and can be valued, you are bonding with future taxpayers.

There has been a lot of research about the teen brain in recent years. We know now, for instance, that the teen brain is still growing and changing rather than already formed. In *The Primal Teen,* Barbara Strauch says,

> The teenage brain, it's now becoming clear, is still very much a work in progress, a giant construction project. Millions of connections are being hooked up; millions more are swept away. Neurochemicals wash over the teenage brain, giving it a new paint job, a new look, a new chance at life. The teenage brain is raw, vulnerable. It's a brain that is becoming what it will be.
>
> "We used to think that, if there were brain changes at all in adolescence, they were subtle," Elizabeth Sowell, a neuroscientist at UCLA and one of the country's top researchers of the adolescent brain, told me. "Now we know that those changes are not as subtle as we thought. Every time we look at another set of teenage brains, we find something new."[1]

If you have never taken a course in developmental or educational psychology, reading some of the new brain research may help you to gain a new appreciation for what teens are going through. YALSA offers an online course called "Pain in the Brain: Adolescent Development and Library Behavior."[2] Watch YALSA's website for information about when the course will be offered next, or get information about licensing the course for your library system.

Beginning in 1989, the Search Institute conducted surveys of sixth through twelfth graders in public and private schools all over the United States. In 1990 they first published their list of forty Developmental Assets for Adolescents, described as "40 common sense, positive experiences and qualities that help influence choices young people make and help them become caring, responsible adults." Their studies have shown that "the more assets young people have, the less likely they are to engage in a wide range of high-risk behaviors and the more likely they are to thrive."[3]

In the twenty years since the assets were first defined, youth-serving professionals of all types, including librarians, have used them as a basis for planning and defending programs for teens. Libraries can provide the "external" assets, like support, empowerment, boundaries and expectations, and constructive use of time. These in turn allow teens to develop the "internal" assets, like commitment to learning, positive values (integrity, honesty, social justice, etc.), social competencies (conflict resolution, planning and decision making, etc.), and positive identity.

In a YALSA "train the trainers" program, program presenters used a list of "Seven Developmental Needs of YAs," based on Gayle Dorman's *The Middle Grades Assessment Program: User's Manual.* (See boxed text, pages 18–19.) This particular list of developmental needs is focused specifically on what teens are going through, physically and emotionally. It also includes a useful list of "contradictions and characteristics" for the teen years: teens can be energetic one moment and lethargic the next, for example.

In 1999 the Wallace Foundation funded the Public Libraries as Partners in Youth Development initiative. The Chapin Hall Center for Children at the University of Chicago presented the findings from the initiative in 2005, in a report entitled *New on the Shelf: Teens in the Library.* This influential report used the language of positive youth development to show how libraries can benefit teens, and how teen services can benefit libraries and communities. Among their findings was the statement that

> Ongoing staff training to build knowledge of youth development and ways of working with teens is an important part of successful youth programming. . . . Emphasizing a youth development approach can be very helpful if it encourages staff to relate to teens in new ways and addresses their practical concerns about working with youth.[4]

As you plan programs and activities, consider which of the Seven Developmental Needs or Search Institute Developmental Assets these programs address. Being aware of youth development serves multiple purposes. Not only will knowledge of developmental needs and assets help you understand the teens you work with and help you know how to respond to them, it will also put you in a position to make the strongest possible case for the programs and activities you want to pursue. For example, if you are proposing that your library create a teen advisory board, you can include in your justification to library administration that it meets multiple youth developmental needs, including empowerment, social competencies, constructive use of time, and positive identity. Administrators and library boards want to know that the library is being used as a positive force in the life of teens, so put the information in front of them.

Look at your current programs and list the developmental needs that are addressed by them. Then look at the lists of developmental needs and make a list of programs and services that might meet those needs. For example, gaming programs, craft programs, film programs, and book-related programs all relate to the need that teens have to develop new interests, understand and accept themselves, and see that others have felt the same emotions, as well as the need to do something well and receive admiration and the need to explore their widening world. Always include information about what needs are being met by any program or service you propose; doing so will strengthen your case and help your entire library community understand teens better.

It is important to realize, and to convey to the rest of the staff, that not all teenagers are alike. The YA librarian needs to have services and collections for the full range of teen ages and interests. Twelve-year-olds are very different from eighteen-year-olds. There are religious teens, nonreligious teens,

Adolescent Development/ Developmental Assets

Seven Developmental Needs of YAs

1. Physical Activity: Teens have boundless energy and dreamy lethargy. YAs have growing bodies and need time to move and relax.

2. Competence and Achievement: YAs are self-conscious about themselves. Teens need to do something well and receive admiration. Teens need chances to prove themselves (to themselves and to others).

3. Self-Definition: YAs need opportunities to explore their widening world. Teens need to reflect upon new experiences and their role. They need chances to explore ethnic and gender identity.

4. Creative Expression: Teens need to express new feelings and interests. This expression helps YAs understand and accept themselves. Exposure to arts shows that others have felt the same emotions new to YAs.

5. Positive Social Interaction with Peers and Adults: Teens need support, companionship, and constructive criticism. YAs need relationships with those willing to share. The family is of primary importance for values.

6. Structure and Clear Limits: Teens need to know and understand the rules of the system. The search for security by teens is helped by having established boundaries. Teens are capable of working with adults to set their own rules.

7. Meaningful Participation: Teens need opportunities in which to express social and intellectual skills. Through participation, teens gain a sense of responsibility. Teens need opportunities to make meaningful contributions to their community.

Contradictions and Characteristics during the Teen Years

Energetic/Lethargic

Arrogant/Low self-esteem

Outrageous/Shy

Smart/Stupid

Always in groups/Loners

Rebellious/Fearful

In your face/On the fringe

Goals during Adolescence

Independence

Excitement

Identity

Acceptance

Based on Gayle Dorman, *The Middle Grades Assessment Program: User's Manual.* Minneapolis, MN: Center for Early Adolescence, 1981.

and plenty of questioning teens. There are teens who are avid readers and teens who can read but just prefer not to. There are teens who are up on all the latest technology and teens who don't even have a cell phone and don't want one. There are teens who like wrestling, teens who like poetry, teens who like country music, teens who like classical music, teens who take school seriously, and teens who are just marking time in class. There are teens with special needs, with physical, mental, and cognitive differences, and the library must serve them. There are teens who are in foster care, in group homes, and in correctional facilities.

Teens are in the process of finding out who they are and what they value. Some already know what they want to do with their lives. We have probably all met the dedicated dancer or musician or athlete or computer geek who is absolutely certain at age fifteen how he or she is going to live, and some of them even succeed at it. Many more are still trying on personalities, figuring out who they are going to become. So it is never a good idea to pigeonhole a teenager. Being aware of some of the research on today's teens will help you get a big picture of your client group.

Today's teens are part of a larger group known as Millennials (those born between 1981 and 2000). The Pew Research Center is in the process of producing a series of original reports that explore the behaviors, values, and opinions of today's teens and twenty-somethings. Here are some of the things they already know about this generation:

- They are the most ethnically and racially diverse cohort of youth in the nation's history. Among those ages thirteen to twenty-nine: 18.5 percent are Hispanic; 14.2 percent are black; 4.3 percent are Asian; 3.2 percent are mixed race or other; and 59.8 percent, a record low, are white.
- They are starting out as the most politically progressive age group in modern history. In the 2008 election, Millennials voted for Barack Obama over John McCain by 66 percent to 32 percent, while adults ages thirty and over split their votes 50 percent to 49 percent. In the four decades since the development of Election Day exit polling, this is the largest gap ever seen in a presidential election between the votes of those under and over age thirty.
- They are the first generation in human history who regard behaviors like tweeting and texting, along with websites like Facebook, YouTube, Google, and Wikipedia, not as astonishing innovations of the digital era, but as everyday parts of their social lives and their search for understanding.
- They are the least religiously observant youths since survey research began charting religious behavior.
- They are more inclined toward trust in institutions than were either of their two predecessor generations—Gen Xers (who are now ages thirty to forty-five) and baby boomers (now ages forty-six to sixty-four) when they were coming of age.[5]

In the fall of 2009, Lee Rainie of the Pew Internet Project made the presentation "Teens in the Digital Age." He made some conclusions about how the digital age has affected the learning styles of today's teens, who are what he calls "networked learners." They are, he says,

- More self-directed and less dependent on top-down instructions
- Better arrayed to capture new information inputs
- More reliant on feedback and response
- More attuned to group outreach and group knowledge
- More open to cross-discipline insights, creating their own "tagged" taxonomies
- More oriented toward people being their own individual nodes of production[6]

Similarly, a research project funded by the MacArthur Foundation in 2008 found that

> The digital world is creating new opportunities for youth to grapple with social norms, explore interests, develop technical skills, and experiment with new forms of self-expression. These activities have captured teens' attention because they provide avenues for extending social worlds, self-directed learning, and independence.[7]

For teens, the library—particularly the public library—can serve the critical role of a "third place," a place that is not school or home, but a separate, social space. It is a place where teens can hang out, meet friends, explore the world, and make contacts with caring adults. The library can assist in this by accepting teenagers, and respecting their space and their opinions. This means working with teens to provide for all of their many and varied interests: books, yes, but also their technological interests. Providing opportunities for gaming, for creating podcasts and videos, and for working on web pages are all ways the library can acknowledge teens' technology interests and developmental needs.

Demonstrating an understanding of and respect for diverse cultural and ethnic values is another way to connect with teens. This goes beyond having diverse materials in the collection. Our libraries are often more diverse than we realize. Just because we don't see people of different cultures in our libraries doesn't mean they are not present in our communities. Why should they come to the library if there is nothing there that reflects their culture or ethnicity? Different cultures also have different ways of using the library. When the Morgan Hill Library in California's Santa Clara County Library system was building a new library in 2007, the staff observed the ways in which the

From "Teenagers, Libraries, the Digital Age"

The prophets of the death of print simply do not know that libraries both allow for teenagers and evolve their services in response to teenagers' interests. They see "digital native" teens as the harbingers of the future, in which books will be gone. But those very teenagers are finding one of the only places that really suits them is one filled with books, devoted to books, staffed by people eager to show them books that they may enjoy, or learn from, or find useful. Sure, you could argue that teenagers just go to the libraries to do digital stuff and socialize, and ignore the books. But that does not seem to be the case. And that is because the libraries are not binary—books or sites, past or future. Rather they offer teenagers many different forms of entertainment and connection, which is exactly what teenagers want.

Marc Aronson, blog post, "Teenagers, Libraries, the Digital Age" www.schoollibrary journal.com/blog/1880000388/post/1010042901.html; used with permission.

city's Hispanic population used the library. They noticed that families came to the library together and moved through the library as a unit, spending time first in the children's area, then moving to the adult Spanish-language area. So when the new library was built, it included a large browsing area, complete with upholstered chairs as well as reading tables, in the middle of a section that contained Spanish-language materials for all ages. The family might still browse in the English-language children's area, but at least while the parents are looking for materials, there is a place for the children to sit, and Spanish-language materials for them to look at.

Again, you can go to the statistics, but this time you will need to look beyond what the library collects. Look at census data for your area and, if possible, find out what the local school districts know about the ethnic and cultural groups in your community. This will give you a starting place to examine your collection and programming. Consider whether your immigrant populations are first, second, or third generation. One library I worked at had a large Japanese-language collection because, historically, the community had included a sizable number of Japanese immigrants. However, by the time I worked there, the first generation was dying off, and the second and third generations, who had grown up in California, did not read Japanese. They were, however, still interested in Japanese culture, and wanted their children to know about where they had originally come from. So we stopped collecting materials in Japanese and focused that money on collecting English-language materials about Japanese culture. Many teens from immigrant households have grown up speaking the language of their parents, but have never learned to read or write in that language, because they have always gone to school in the United States. They may, however, very much enjoy listening to music or watching movies in that language. Consider these factors when purchasing materials.

Read what the teens are reading. Read the latest, hottest book, the book they are all passing around, even if you don't think you will like it. You might be surprised, and you will certainly learn something about the teens in your community and what they find appealing. And don't stop with books. Keep your eye out for anything having to do with teen culture. Read magazines, read newspapers, read blogs, pay attention to new research about teens. The Pew Research Center, as noted above, is an excellent source of information about all aspects of teen life. You can get an e-mail newsletter or add their bulletins to your RSS feed aggregator.

Most of all, listen to the teens in your community. The easiest place to start is with the teens who are already in your library. When they come to you for help, engage them in conversation. Find out what they are studying and what they think about it. If you help them find a book, ask them to come back and let you know how they liked it. Be open to their reading suggestions,

Creating music is a very popular activity at my library in Charlotte, North Carolina. The music the teens make is different than what I usually listen to. My library branch serves urban teens, and rap music is by far the most popular genre of music that is created. We have developed programs such as open mic nights and opportunities for teens to learn more about rap music because it is so popular here. Because I hear it so often, although I'm certainly no expert, I definitely have a better appreciation for the music. Our policies for what is and isn't appropriate to be sung aims to take into account that the teens are saying something very important to them yet they might need some suggestions for alternate words so that everyone can feel safe and respected in the facility.

Kelly Czarnecki
Technology Education Librarian
ImaginOn, Charlotte Mecklenburg (North Carolina) Library

and follow up with them, by letting them know what you thought of a book they recommended.

But don't stop with the teens in your library. Look to the rest of your community, and come up with some ways to connect and learn more about your local teens. Some suggestions for how to do this are in chapter 3.

SUGGESTED READING

Agosto, Denise E., and Sandra Hughes-Hassell, eds. *Urban Teens in the Library: Research and Practice.* Chicago: American Library Association, 2009.

Alexander, Linda B., and Nahyun Kwon, for YALSA. *Multicultural Programs for Tweens and Teens.* Chicago: American Library Association, 2010.

Anderson, Sheila B. *Extreme Teens: Library Services to Nontraditional Young Adults.* Westport, CT: Libraries Unlimited, 2005.

Anderson, Sheila B. *Serving Older Teens.* Westport, CT: Libraries Unlimited, 2003.

Anderson, Sheila B. *Serving Young Teens and 'Tweens.* Westport, CT: Libraries Unlimited, 2007.

Brehm-Heeger, Paula. "Blurring the Lines: Urban Library Problems Have Gone Suburban." *School Library Journal* 54, no. 10:29.

Brehm-Heeger, Paula. *Serving Urban Teens.* Westport, CT: Libraries Unlimited, 2008.

Burek Pierce, Jennifer. *Sex, Brains, and Video Games: The Librarian's Guide to Teens in the Twenty-first Century.* Chicago: American Library Association, 2007.

Carman, L. Kay, and Carol S. Reich. *Reaching Out to Religious Youth: A Guide to Services, Programs, and Collections.* Westport, CT: Libraries Unlimited, 2004.

Gorman, Michele. "Stir It Up." *School Library Journal* 52, no. 2:35.

Gorman, Michele. "The 'Terrible Teens.'" *School Library Journal* 52, no. 6:34.

Ito, Mizuko, Sonja Baumer, Matteo Bittanti, danah boyd, Rachel Cody, Becky Herr-Stephenson, Heather A. Horst, et al. *Hanging Out, Messing Around, and Geeking Out: Kids Living and Learning with New Media.* Cambridge, MA: MIT Press, 2009.

Ito, Mizuko, Michael Carter, and Barrie Thorne. "Kids' Informal Learning with Digital Media: An Ethnographic Investigation of Innovative Knowledge Cultures." http://digitalyouth.ischool.berkeley.edu.

Keeter, Scott, and Paul Taylor. "The Millennials." Pew Research Center. http://pewresearch.org/pubs/1437/millennials-profile.

Martin, Hillias J., and James R. Murdock. *Serving Lesbian, Gay, Bisexual, Transgender, and Questioning Teens: A How-to-Do-It Manual for Librarians.* New York: Neal-Schuman Publishers, 2007.

O'Dell, Katie. *Library Materials and Services for Teen Girls.* Westport, CT: Libraries Unlimited, 2002.

Spielberger, Julie, Carol Horton, Lisa Michels, and Robert Halpern. *New on the Shelf: Teens in the Library.* Chicago: Chapin Hall Center for Children at the University of Chicago, 2005. www.chapinhall.org/research/report/new-shelf.

Strauch, Barbara. *The Primal Teen.* New York: Doubleday, 2003.

University of Arizona Library. "Needs Assessment Tutorial." http://digital.library
.arizona.edu/nadm/tutorial/resources_2.htm.

Welch, Rollie J. *The Guy-Friendly YA Library: Serving Male Teens.* Westport, CT:
Libraries Unlimited, 2007.

NOTES

1. Barbara Strauch, *The Primal Teen* (New York: Doubleday, 2003), 8.
2. YALSA Online Courses. www.ala.org/onlinecourses/.
3. Search Institute, "What Kids Need: Developmental Assets." www.search-institute.org/
developmental-assets.
4. Julie Spielberger, Carol Horton, Lisa Michels, and Robert Halpern, *New on the Shelf:
Teens in the Library* (Chicago: Chapin Hall Center for Children at the University of
Chicago, 2005). www.chapinhall.org/research/report/new-shelf.
5. Pew Research Center, "Millennials: A Portrait of Generation Next." www.pewresearch
.org/pubs/1437/millennials-profile.
6. Lee Rainie, "Networked Learners." www.pewinternet.org/Presentations/2009/52
-Networked-Learners.aspx.
7. Mizuko Ito, Heather Horst, Matteo Bittanti, danah boyd, Becky Herr-Stephenson,
Patricia G. Lange, C. J. Pascoe, and Laura Robinson, *Living and Learning with New Media:
Summary of Findings from the Digital Youth Project* (Digital Youth Research, 2008). http://
digitalyouth.ischool.berkeley.edu/files/report/digitalyouth-TwoPageSummary.pdf.

chapter THREE

COMPETENCY AREA III
Communication, Marketing, and Outreach

THE LIBRARIAN will be able to:

1. Form appropriate professional relationships with young adults, providing them with the assets, inputs, and resiliency factors that they need to develop into caring, competent adults.

2. Develop relationships and partnerships with young adults, administrators, and other youth-serving professionals in the community by establishing regular communication and by taking advantage of opportunities to meet in person.

3. Be an advocate for young adults and effectively promote the role of the library in serving young adults, demonstrating that the provision of services to this group can help young adults build assets, achieve success, and, in turn, create a stronger community.

4. Design, implement, and evaluate a strategic marketing plan for promoting young adult services in the library, schools, youth-serving agencies, and the community at large.

5. Demonstrate the capacity to articulate relationships between young adult services and the parent institution's core goals and mission.

6. Establish an environment in the library wherein all staff serve young adults with courtesy and respect, and all staff are encouraged to promote programs and services for young adults.

7. Identify young adult interests and groups underserved or not yet served by the library, including at-risk teens, those with disabilities, non–English speakers, etc., as well as those with special or niche interests.

8. Promote young adult library services directly to young adults through school visits, library tours, etc., and through engaging their parents, educators, and other youth-serving community partners.

In chapter 2, we looked at the developmental needs of teens. By forming appropriate relationships with young adults, the YA librarian can provide them with some of the factors they need to develop into caring, competent adults. Review the forty Developmental Assets for Adolescents, focusing on the first twenty. Many of the support factors involve the teen's parents, but teens also need support from nonparent adults. The library can take a large part in empowerment, showing the teen that adults in the community (e.g., the YA librarian) value youth participation in the library and the community. The library may be a place where the teen can volunteer time to assist in a wide variety of programs and projects. Likewise, the librarian can model appropriate behavior for the teen.

As a young adult librarian, it is easy to focus only on the teens. After all, they are in front of you every day, with their needs, their wants, and their demands for attention. And teens are important, of course. But in order to serve teens really well, it is critical to build and maintain relationships with a variety of other groups, including other library or school staff, your super-visors, your community's leaders, and other youth-serving professionals in your area.

Start with your library, and your supervisor. Even if—especially if—your supervisor gives you a completely free hand with what you do in the YA department, be sure you keep him or her in the loop. Suggest regular meet-ings, if they don't already exist, and make sure your supervisor knows about your upcoming plans for programs, services, and collections. The children's department should also be kept apprised of what is going on in the teen area. In many libraries, there is overlap at the middle school age range ('tweens)

Project Payoff

When teens have fines on their accounts that prohibit them from using the library resources, we work with them to help them reduce those fines while they utilize the library. "Project Payoff" is a program that allows teens to reduce their fines by five dollars for every one hour that they read at the library or attend a program at the library. We understand that teens often accumulate fines on their accounts before they understand the way a library works, and often they note that their parents or siblings actually took out materials using their cards and that was the cause of the fines. When we talk to teens about "Project Payoff" we have the opportunity to educate them about library fines and how to avoid fines on their accounts. Teens are always glad when we tell them about the program because during the three-month period that they are in the "Project Payoff" program, they are able to check out a limited number of materials and use library computers. For example, recently a teen told me she couldn't use the computer because of fines. I told her about the program we have that will enable her to read down her fines. She was impressed and thought it was really "cool." "Project Payoff" allows us to help teens remain active, lifelong library patrons.

Michele Gorman
Teen Services Coordinator
Charlotte Mecklenburg (North Carolina) Library

between children's and YA. If there is a children's librarian who may be planning programs or services for middle schoolers, the two of you need to be talking.

Identify key staff members who are teen advocates. Is your director or assistant director a former YA librarian? Does your branch manager have teenage children? These people might be your supporters when you want to propose a new program or service. Don't forget about support staff. A circulation clerk with an interest in teens can be a great ally in getting the message across to other clerks. Pages, especially ones who are in high school and college, can be great sources of information about the community and what resources it already offers for teens. Make it your business to talk to all of these people and let them know what you are planning.

Provide library staff with the tools they need to promote programs and services for young adults. They may well be able to help you in some way

Creating a Safe and Inviting Space for Teens in Our Community

We understand that some of the teens who hang out at the Loft at ImaginOn may not always have an inviting place to go after school where they can feel safe. We strive to create that place for them here by asking all teens to adhere to three simple rules: "Respect Yourself, Respect Others, Respect the Space." Below are two examples of the feedback we received from teens who enjoy the space. Upon seeing a teen who had not been to the Loft in a week, a Loft staff member said, "Where have you been, man?" in a friendly way. The teen said that he was sorry that he hadn't shown up, and somewhere in the conversation he mentioned that ImaginOn was his second home and the staff here are his second family. Another time, a teen wrote a G.E.M. (an acknowledgment that a staff member has "Gone the Extra Mile" for a patron) for the staff of the Loft to say how grateful he is that the staff are always around to help him with library-related issues, as well as to talk to him about everyday issues in his life, such as his arguments with his mother.

Michele Gorman
Teen Services Coordinator
Charlotte Mecklenburg (North Carolina) Library

you haven't even thought of. Circulation desk staff should have fliers and handouts about teen programs that they can share with teens and parents who are checking out materials. The more you work with staff and help them see how the YA program fits into the bigger picture of the library's mission, the more helpful they will be. Acknowledge and thank staff when you see them interacting in positive ways with teens. Talk to your supervisor or director and find out if you can be part of the formal training or orientation program for all new staff members. This will give you an opportunity to share with new staff your vision of YA services and convey the message that teens deserve the same level of courtesy and respect that all other patrons do.

Next, think about the community at large. Start by making a list of teen-serving agencies and organizations in your community—schools, parks and recreation, YMCA, youth centers, Scouts. Find out actual names and contact information. Even if you do nothing about this right away, these names may come in handy in the future. Find out what kinds of programs for youth are offered in your community. Is there a citywide youth advisory board? Does the recreation center or YMCA have special programs for teens? Look for ways

The biggest partnership/collaboration project I do is TBF Live: The Greater Rochester Teen Book Festival, which I founded in 2006. Three counties, two library systems, and school and public librarians working together ... and now we are hosted in a local college and supported by their education department. We have also begun to offer space at the festival for other teen-focused organizations, with this coming year featuring Melissa's Living Legacy and their new Center for Teens Coping with Cancer.

Stephanie A. Squicciarini, MLS
Teen/Young Adult Services Librarian
Fairport (New York) Public Library

to integrate these programs with library services. Attend community meetings for organizations serving teens and brainstorm possible collaborations. Keep the developmental assets in mind when coming up with ideas. The Chapin Hall discussion paper *New on the Shelf: Teens in the Library* points out that "the language of youth development helps to connect public libraries to a larger network of youth organizations and policy discussions."[1]

Know who your local elected and appointed officials and staff are (mayor, city manager, city council, county board of supervisors, school board, etc.). Find out if any of them have teenagers at home. This can sometimes be a toe in the door for you to connect with them. Offer to meet with city staff and elected officials, either individually or at a formal meeting. Come prepared with a brief (one- or two-minute) speech about what is going on in teen services, and bring handouts. Most public bodies (city councils, school boards, library boards, etc.) begin their meetings with a time for public comment. Usually remarks in this time period are limited to three minutes. That can be a good time to get a brief message out to the community about what you are doing with and for teens in the library. Don't use this time to ask for anything, just give a positive, upbeat message. If you do this a few times a year, it will put the idea of your program into their minds, which can be useful when it is time for budget allocations. When you do have something specific to ask for, whether it is a proclamation for Teen Read Week or a budget allocation, they will already be familiar with you and your program. As always, be sure your supervisor and your director are in the loop; they may have political reasons for you to wait a week or a month.

Proclamations and news releases are good ways to get positive information about teens and libraries out to the public and your local elected officials. YALSA provides valuable publicity tools such as sample proclamations, news releases, letters to the editor, and public service announcements for its programs and initiatives, like the Youth Media Awards, Teen Read Week™, and Teen Tech Week™. These events, as well as others like the announcement of YALSA's book and media awards every January, the Teens' Top Ten in October, and Summer Reading Program in June or July, can be great opportunities for you to share positive information with your community about teens and how they use the library. When you have developed contacts both in and outside of the library, you can use them to add punch to your news releases: quoting the mayor in your news release may encourage the local newspaper to pick up the story.

If you have an opportunity to make a formal presentation to a library board, a city council, or a school board, concentrate on being concise and positive, and focus on how your programs achieve the goals that you and the library have set. Before you even begin planning your presentation, review your YA strategic plan, the parent institution's strategic plan, and the goals and objectives of the department, the library, and, if possible, the larger community (city, county, school district). Show how your programs and services align with the library's goals as well as how they move forward the goals of the community. (See chapter 4 for more information on strategic plans.)

Meet with school leaders (principals, librarians, school boards). Discuss how you and they can work together to achieve your goals. The YALSA Professional Development Center includes information on school-library partnerships online at www.ala.org/ala/yalsa/profdev/schoolpublic.htm. These are actual programs that real school and public libraries are cooperating on, complete with contact information to find out more details.

One key to communicating with a wide range of people in the community is to have a clear idea of what it is you do and what you are trying to achieve. Come up with a series of "elevator speeches." These are brief (thirty seconds or so) statements about what you do and why it matters. It's the sort of thing you could say if you met a mover and shaker in an elevator and only had the time of the elevator ride to get your point across. You can make up elevator speeches about any aspect of teen services, but it is always useful to be clear about how teen services mesh with the goals and mission of the library and the community. Tell a story that shows something positive about the teenagers in your library. Here is an example:

> My passion is working with teenagers to help them become caring, responsible adults. We do that here at the library not just by having activities for teens, but by getting teens involved in the planning process. We've got a great group of teens who are really becoming leaders. Have you seen the YouTube video they made to promote the library? When I look at these kids, I have no worries about the future of this town.

I often advocate for teen involvement in the library and community by partnering with other local governmental and nonprofit organizations. This both supports teen involvement in the broader community and helps make the library visible as a space that seeks and welcomes teen involvement. Both the city of Portland, Oregon, and Multnomah County are models for effective, progressive youth involvement. The City/County Youth Engagement Team has representation from the joint City/County policy advisory body, the Multnomah Youth Commission, the Youth Planner Program in the City of Portland's Bureau of Planning and Sustainability, Multnomah County's School-Based Health Center program, the City of Portland Parks and Recreation, and Multnomah County Libraries Teen Programs. Our work is guided by "Our Bill of Rights: Children + Youth," the nation's first Bill of Rights written by and for young people and adopted by a local government. (Visit http://bit.ly/7BOjsb for background on the bill of rights.)

As a concrete example of how this partnering works, this week I'm serving on a hiring panel for the position of Youth Development Coordinator, the county staff member whose role is to advise (but not direct!) the Youth Commission in their work. The panel includes youth commissioners as well as adults from other city and county departments that support strong youth involvement. The youth commissioners are taking the lead in interviewing the candidates, and it's inspiring to see the passion, intelligence, and commitment the youth commissioners are bringing to the task.

Sara Ryan
Teen Services Specialist
Multnomah County Library, Portland, Oregon, and board of directors, YALSA

Advocating for teens can take many different forms. In chapter 1, we discussed ways to ensure that teens have their fair share of the budget. In chapter 4, we will look at how library policies and procedures can support young adults. In considering taking your message about teen services to the public, look at some of the resources that YALSA offers for advocacy. A good place to start is "Speaking Up for Library Services to Teens: A Guide to Advocacy" (www.ala.org/ala/mgrps/divs/yalsa/advocacy_final.pdf). It contains tips on how to start advocating, and tools to make it easier. It includes information on marketing and media relations, and detailed information on legislative advocacy. The tools will help you prepare an action plan and create a message. Explore these resources and determine what you can do in the next month, six months, year, or two years. YALSA's wiki has many more resources for advocacy, including the "YA Advocacy Action Plan Workbook," to help you get started advocating for teens in libraries.[2]

Again, don't forget to involve teens in your advocacy messages. They can be some of your most potent resources. An example of this is Oakland (California) Public Library's Youth Leadership Council. The YLC is comprised of "active teens (thirteen through nineteen) determined to improve the libraries of Oakland." What they do is "gain communication skills, public speaking skills, self-confidence, leadership experience, ins and outs of event planning and friends! Directly interact with high level community leaders and participate in local and national functions."[3] At the ALA Annual Conference in Anaheim in 2008, the teens appeared on a panel and shared how they had gone to Sacramento to participate in Library Legislative Day and met with state senators and assembly members to advocate for libraries. (See boxed text, page 35.) They have also presented issues and concerns to the city's library board and represented the library at community events.

Consider creating a YA e-mail newsletter or blog to share information. You could include information on upcoming programs, reviews of new books, information about volunteer opportunities, and so on. If you push it out as an e-mail newsletter, be sure to include teens, parents, library staff, and your community partners. If you create a blog, send out occasional e-mail teasers to draw people to the site. Twitter and Facebook are other good ways to let people know when you are updating.

Explore social networking sites as a means of outreach to teens, including those who are not current library users. Look at YALSA's "Teens and Social Networking in School and Public Libraries Toolkit" for some ideas; it contains examples of thirty positive uses of social networking.[4] Find out what other libraries are doing with Facebook, MySpace, and Twitter, among other sites, and make a plan for how you can use these tools to communicate with your teens, with their parents, and with the community at large.

There are many unserved and underserved groups of teens in your community. At-risk teens, foster teens, teens with disabilities, teens in juvenile detention facilities, and non–English speakers are some of these. Look at your community and identify some of these groups, and then brainstorm what you might do to provide them with library services. You may not be able to accomplish everything, but you may find that there are ways to improve service that fit into your library's plan and budget.

Communication and outreach are critical to your success in serving teens. The relationships you build with teens, with library staff members, and with the community will make your program stronger and help you build your case for improved funding and more services. Promoting the role of the library in the lives of teens and the role of teens in the life of the library and the community will help make your program an integral part of the community,

Fostering Youth Advocacy: How Libraries Can Help

As future-driven librarians it is our responsibility to build positive, life-enriching practices that better serve our youth populations. Within ten years, these marvelous teens here in front of us will be our doctors, our lawyers, and our library stakeholders. Acting as guides and mentors, it is imperative that librarians and educators empower and engage our youth to be well-informed, self-determined citizens through providing them with a platform and a voice. That is the purpose of starting a youth leadership council at your library. I am proud to say that Oakland Public Library was in the forefront of prioritizing the need to partner with teens while engaging them in civic responsibility. Within the scope of mentor, educator, and youth advocate, teen librarians can arm our youth with the skill-set they require to participate fully, articulately, and intelligently in their government at the local, state, and national level so as to ensure the satisfaction of their and our needs within a healthy society. Starting at the library level teens can be on the library board, they can advocate and educate around library bond measures, and they can act as ambassadors for the library. Oakland's teens have provided input on facility master plans, they have attended and spoken at city council meetings, they annually attend Library Legislation Day at the state capitol where they speak with state representatives and the State Librarian.

I learned when I started a group at my prior job in North Carolina that teens are very eager to get involved and have a chance to speak up. It's easy to start your own group. Just invite some kids, bring the pizza, present a few guidelines, and step out of their way. The teens will shine.

Jodi Mitchell
Teen Outreach Librarian and YLC Coordinator
Oakland (California) Public Library

will help teens grow into successful adults, and will help your community grow stronger.

SUGGESTED READING

ALA Advocacy Resource Center. www.ala.org/ala/issuesadvocacy.
ALA Legislative Action Center. http://capwiz.com/ala/home.
ALA Office for Library Advocacy. www.ala.org/ola.

Braun, Linda W. "I Wish I'd Said." www.voya.com/2010/03/30/tag-team-tech/#section17.

Brehm-Heeger, Paula. "Better Late Than Never." *School Library Journal* 53, no. 2:30.

Brehm-Heeger, Paula. "What's Going On?" *School Library Journal* 54, no. 2:27.

Gilman, Isaac. "Beyond Books: Restorative Librarianship in Juvenile Detention Centers." *Public Libraries* 47, no. 1:59–66.

Ratledge, Alyssa. "One Teen among Adults on the Library Board." *Voice of Youth Advocates* 30, no. 4:313.

Rockefeller, Elsworth. "Striving to Serve Diverse Youth: Mainstreaming Teens with Special Needs through Public Library Programming." *Public Libraries* 47, no. 1:50–55.

Spielberger, Julie, Carol Horton, Lisa Michels, and Robert Halpern. *New on the Shelf: Teens in the Library—Findings from the Evaluation of Public Libraries as Partners in Youth Development.* www.chapinhall.org/research/report/new-shelf.

Suellentrop, Tricia. "Letting Go." *School Library Journal* 52 no. 5:39.

Suellentrop, Tricia. "Moving on Up." *School Library Journal* 53 no. 4:32.

Suellentrop, Tricia. "The Party Poopers." *School Library Journal* 54 no. 12:23.

Tuccillo, Diane P. "Standing Room Only: Want to Get Teens Excited about the Library? Just Surrender Some Control." *School Library Journal* 53, no. 3:46.

Valenza, Joyce. "High School Seniors and Social Networking." www.voya .com/2010/03/30/tag-team-tech/#section8.

Wendt, Ma'Lis, and Ian Rosenoir. "YALSA @ Your Library®." *Young Adult Library Services* 6, no. 3:10–12.

YALSA. "Advocacy Toolkit." http://wikis.ala.org/yalsa/index.php/Advocating_for_ Teen_Services_in_Libraries.

YALSA. "A Legislative Advocacy Guide for Members." www.ala.org/ala/mgrps/ divs/yalsa/profdev/LegAdvocacyGuide.pdf.

YALSA. "Speaking Up for Library Services to Teens." www.ala.org/ala/mgrps/divs/ yalsa/advocacy_final.pdf.

YALSA. "Teens and Social Networking in School and Public Libraries." www.ala .org/ala/mgrps/divs/yalsa/profdev/socialnetworkingtool.pdf.

NOTES

1. Julie Spielberger, Carol Horton, Lisa Michels, and Robert Halpern, *New on the Shelf: Teens in the Library—Findings from the Evaluation of Public Libraries as Partners in Youth Development.* www.chapinhall.org/research/report/new-shelf:7.
2. YALSA, "The YA Advocacy Action Plan Workbook." http://yalsa.ala.org/presentations/ AdvocacyWorkbook.pdf; YALSA, "Advocating for Teen Services in Libraries." http://wikis.ala.org/yalsa/index.php/Advocating_for_Teen_Services_in_Libraries.
3. Oakland Public Library, "Youth Leadership Council." www.oaklandlibrary.org/links/ teens/ylc.html.
4. YALSA. "Teens and Social Networking in School and Public Libraries." www.ala.org/ ala/mgrps/divs/yalsa/profdev/socialnetworkingtool.pdf.

chapter FOUR

COMPETENCY AREA IV
Administration

THE LIBRARIAN will be able to:

1. Develop a strategic plan for library service with young adults based on their unique needs.

    a. Design and conduct a community analysis and needs assessment.
    b. Apply research findings toward the development and improvement of young adult library services.
    c. Design activities to involve young adults in planning and decision making.

2. Develop, justify, administer, and evaluate a budget for young adult services.

3. Develop physical facilities dedicated to the achievement of young adult service goals.

4. Develop written policies that mandate the rights of young adults to equitable library service.

5. Design, implement, and evaluate an ongoing program of professional development for all staff, to encourage and inspire continual excellence in service to young adults.

6. Identify and defend resources (staff, materials, facilities, funding) that will improve library service to young adults.

7. Document young adult programs and activities so as to contribute to institutional and professional memory.

8. Develop and manage services that utilize the skills, talents, and resources of young adults in the school or community.

Many frontline young adult librarians do not think of themselves as administrators or managers. But having administrative and management skills are vital to having a healthy teen services department. And speaking "management speak" can only help you in accomplishing your goals, because if you want to make changes, at some point you are going to have to make your case to a supervisor, a manager, possibly even a library board. So the more you take a leadership role now, the better prepared you will be to make that presentation. And one more thing: if you hone your administrative and managerial skills now, you will be in a position later to move up into a managerial position. A library director who was once a young adult librarian can be the best possible advocate for teen services.

Whether or not your library has a strategic plan in place, it will be useful for you to develop such a plan for young adult services. But first, find out if your library or school has a strategic plan, and if so what it says (or doesn't say) about young adult services. Whenever possible, in preparing your strategic plan, make it fit into the library's overall plan. In developing a strategic plan for young adult services, you will be more likely to get the buy-in of administration if your plan matches what the library has already stated as its plan. For example, the boxed text on page 39 shows the Santa Clara County (California) Library strategic plan. Its core purpose and core values apply as much to services for young adults as to any other library user.

If you are preparing a YA services strategic plan for a library that already has a plan, you do not need to start from scratch. You just need to come up with some specific strategies that go along with the goals of your institution. In the Santa Clara County example, take the three goal areas and substitute the word "teens" for the phrase "service area residents" and spend some time thinking about how you could accomplish that. What do you need to do to ensure that "more teens use the library as a result of added convenience"? Make a list of things that would make the library's services more convenient

Santa Clara County Library
Strategic Plan

CORE IDEOLOGY

Core Purpose
To enable unbiased, informed, and free access to information, entertainment, and ideas.

Core Organizational Values
- Committed to a positive patron experience.
- Respects the individual and provides quality services in a nonjudgmental way.
- Promotes the love of books and the importance of reading.
- Ensures equal and open access to one relevant, diverse, and substantial collection for the entire community.
- Fosters lifelong learning, promotes cultural enrichment, and supports education.
- Recognizes and respects staff as valuable and essential to quality library services today and into the future.
- Welcomes volunteers and appreciates their contributions of time and talent.
- Ensures that physical spaces are welcoming, safe, clean, and accessible.
- Committed to intellectual freedom and the privacy rights of all patrons.

Goal Area: Convenience
Goal Statement: More service area residents use the library as a result of added convenience.

Goal Area: Public Awareness and Marketing
Goal Statement: More service area residents recognize the library as relevant to their lives.

Goal Area: Information Literacy
Goal Statement: More service area residents choose the library as their trusted source for free, high-quality information.

for teens. Obviously, in some cases you won't be able to do it on your own. It may be more convenient for teens if the library were open every day from two o'clock to midnight, instead of being open in the morning while they're at school and closing at six or nine p.m., just when they're ready to study, but that is not going to be your call. But there are other conveniences that would be more easily achieved. Perhaps one of your goals would be to create a fine-amnesty program (see the boxed text on page 29), so that having overdue items never keeps a teen from being able to check out materials. Think of a list of ways you can bring the library to the teens.

This type of exercise will work for any library's strategic plan. If your library does not have one, you can still make one for the young adult department. To see one example of a complete strategic plan, including strategies, look at YALSA's plan: www.tinyurl.com/yalsastratplan.

In developing a strategic plan, you will want to start by knowing where you are and where you want to go. See chapter 1 for some ideas about using library statistics. You may also want to go over the questions that the PLDS used for their survey in 2007. See if you can find the answers for all of these questions for your library:

- *How does your library define "young adult"?* YALSA says ages twelve through eighteen, but your library may have a different age range.
- *How many young adults used your public library in the past year?* There are different ways to get this number. The simplest is to count the number of twelve- through eighteen-year-olds who have active library cards. You might be able to get a number of young adults who actually checked out at least one item during the year. Neither of these numbers, of course, would reflect the number of YAs without cards who use the library to study, attend programs, etc.
- *What is the young adult population for your library's legal service area?* This will most likely be U.S. Census data. Your director might have the information.
- *How many librarians and/or paraprofessionals (actual persons) are dedicated to young adult services according to their job description in the hours between three in the afternoon and closing?*
- *What is the full-time equivalent for librarians and/or paraprofessionals dedicated to young adult services?*
- *Are your young adult materials maintained in a distinct area (i.e., separate from children's and adult materials) in the central/main branch? In other branches?*

- *What is the total circulation (including renewals) of all young adult materials in all formats?*
- *Do you account for young adult materials separately in your annual materials expenditures? What are your actual expenditures for the current fiscal year?*
- *Does your library have a teen advisory board (or boards)?*
- *Do classes from middle/high schools in your service area come to the public library for visits or instruction?*
- *Do librarians from the public library visit middle/high schools in your service area at least once each academic year?*
- *Are collections shared between school and public library?*
- *Do you collaborate with middle/high schools in your service area when it comes to purchasing materials?*
- *Do you work with youth organizations (4-H, Scouts, etc.) in planning cooperative activities/programs or in providing information/meeting spaces for young adults?*
- *Do you work with cultural organizations (museums, etc.) in planning cooperative activities/programs or in providing information/meeting spaces for young adults?*
- *Do you work with recreational organizations (YMCA, etc.) in planning cooperative activities/programs or in providing information/meeting spaces for young adults?*
- *Do you work with health/mental health organizations in planning cooperative activities/programs or in providing information/meeting spaces for young adults?*
- *How many young adult volunteers have you had in the past year?*
- *In the past year, has your library offered programs geared toward young adults?*
- *How many?*
- *What is the annual attendance for all young adult programs in the past year?*
- *Does your library website have a specific section for young adults?*

The answers to these questions will help you to design and conduct a community analysis and needs assessment. You will of course focus on the young adult portion of your service area. You should be aware that your legal service area may be different from the actual teens served. In a school, it is simple—your school census is your legal service area. But in public libraries, there can be crossover. For example, in many urban areas, there may be a city library as well as a county library. Your patrons may use both libraries, or they may use the one that is most convenient for them. In terms of appealing to your director and your library board, especially if money is involved, you need to be clear about whether you are proposing services that will go to the people whose taxes pay for those services, or whether others are included.

You should certainly involve teens in the analysis and needs assessment process. If you already have a teen advisory board, you will want to include them in the discussion. If not, this may be a good time to start one. But be sure you go beyond polling the teens who already use the library. One way to reach teens who never come to the library is through their schools. If you can get, for example, all of the tenth-grade English teachers to hand out a survey to their classes, you will have a much broader range of responses than if you just hand out surveys in the library. Remember to include private schools as well as public schools. Consider using one of the online survey tools, like Survey Monkey (www.surveymonkey.com), Survey Gizmo (www.surveygizmo .com), or Zoomerang (www.zoomerang.com). Basic versions of these tools are available for free, while more advanced versions require a subscription.

If your library can afford a consultant to conduct a needs assessment, that may carry more weight with your library board or other funders. However, you can learn how to conduct a community analysis and needs assessment yourself, by reading books on the topic, or by checking out an online tutorial, such as the one by the University of Arizona Library (http://digital.library .arizona.edu/nadm/tutorial/resources_2.htm). For examples of library needs assessments, look at the California State Library's list of projects funded by the Library Bond Act of 2000 (www.library.ca.gov/lba2000/fundedprojectslist .html). Each project was required to have an up-to-date community needs assessment, and these are linked on the website. The styles vary, but you will see some of the common elements and get some ideas of what to ask, and how to express your findings.

Next think about writing a mission statement for your YA department, if you don't already have one. As with the strategic plan, go first to your parent organization. What is the library's mission statement? It may be part of the strategic plan, or it may be separate. Make sure that the mission statement you create for young adult services meshes with the library's. For examples of mission statements and statements of philosophy of young adult services, see the boxed text on pages 43–45.

Now go through your library's written policy manual. Do policies and procedures maintain the rights of young adults to equitable library service? As noted in chapter 1, library administrators are not necessarily hostile to the idea of equitable access for teens; they just may never have realized that their policies don't always provide it. Not all policies must be or will be the same for everyone, but here are some areas you might want to examine:

Akron-Summit County (Ohio) Public Library

Mission Statement for the Library

The Akron-Summit County Public Library provides resources for learning and leisure, information services, meeting spaces, and programs for all ages that support, improve, and enrich individual, family, and community life.

Mission Statement for the Teen Department

Akron-Summit County Public Library provides customized library services that connect teens to their local community and the larger world.

- Does your library have policies that are applied only to teen patrons (e.g., noise policies, behavior policies, policies about the number of people that can be at a table, etc.)? Is the policy itself the problem, or is it being enforced inequitably?
- Does your library require parental permission for teens to use certain parts of the collection? Find out what the policy is based on. Is it state law? The interpretation of the library's attorney? The library board's decision? Can the policy be changed?
- What are your library's policies regarding computer and Internet access? Do teens have the same time limits as everyone else? Are teens limited to filtered computers? Again, find out the basis of this policy, and determine whether it can be changed to make teen access more equitable.
- What is your library's policy about volunteers? Does it apply to teens as well as to adults?
- Are circulation policies equitable? Are there different borrowing periods or fines for teen materials?
- Is a driver's license or other formal identification card required to obtain a library card? Are there other options for minors who don't have this type of ID?
- Does the library need new policies that specifically relate to service to teens?

Talk to the teens who use your library. Find out from them if they are aware of library policies that discriminate against them. Teens are usually acutely aware of injustice, but they are also learning to take responsibility for their

Mariposa County (California) Library Young Adult Services

Mission Statement

Mariposa County Library is committed to supporting the special needs of the young adult population of Mariposa County. The library strives to enrich the lives of young adults by meeting their informational, recreational, and cultural needs. Library services are provided by a helpful, caring staff who pay attention to young adults and support their creative needs. We promote and provide free access to all library materials, including electronic resources.

Long-Range Goals for Young Adult Library Services

Expand the young adult collection and services
- Add a music collection
- Increase magazine collection
- Increase classic fiction, popular fiction, and popular nonfiction
- Designate YA areas in branches

Seek cooperation with local schools
- Communicate regularly with local school librarians and teachers

Enhance library services through input from and cooperation with local young adult groups and interested individuals
- Create a Youth Advisory Board with regular meetings
- Better define YA area by moving parts of the collection and some furniture, and add posters and décor chosen by YAs

Involve local young adults in collection development
- Distribute a magazine survey
- Use Youth Advisory Board suggestions
- Develop a music collection

Invite advice from local young adults, via informal and formal user surveys and direct communication, on how to make the library more useful and young adult-friendly
- Distribute a user survey
- Maintain a suggestion box for YAs

Encourage local young adults to work as volunteers at the library, possibly in assisting patrons in the use of the Internet, word processing, and the online card catalog
- Investigate development of a program in which YAs would do volunteer work (possibly with school credit) as technology assistants

www.mariposalibrary.org/services-youngadult.php.

Santa Clara County (California) Library

Philosophy of Teen Services

As librarians, we are committed to helping everyone find recreational, informational, and educational resources in the public library. Special attention and services are due to teens because:

- Studies consistently indicate that at least 23 percent of library users are teens.
- The library is in a unique position to offer information in a non-judgmental way, and to support teens as they experience adolescence.
- Some of the materials most meaningful to teens are of little interest to other age groups.
- The perennial "generation gap" and consequent communication problems often make it difficult for teens to obtain desired services from libraries.
- Many teens use the library only for homework purposes and need to be encouraged to become lifelong users.
- It is important to win the support of teens, who are tomorrow's taxpayers and voters.

At Santa Clara County Library, we recognize that in order to help teens attain adulthood, a wide variety of materials and services must be available. Items of interest should be purchased in quantities to meet demand. Controversial materials that challenge commonly accepted ideas might be particularly important to young people who are learning to make life decisions and should be included in the collection. The right of each teen to have unrestricted access to all parts of the library's collection is affirmed.

Teen librarians believe that reading enriches people's lives and they will creatively promote this important and enjoyable activity.

actions. Involving teens in creating the rules and the consequences for breaking rules will help to give them a sense of ownership and responsibility.

Once you have examined the existing policies, you can make suggestions for changes. As with any proposal to administration, you will want to proceed with deliberation. Understand the basis for the policies as they currently exist. Learn the process for changing policies; find out who must approve any policy changes. In one library system I worked for, policy changes could be proposed by anyone, but had to be reviewed by the service group (adult/teen managers, children's managers, circulation managers) that would be most affected by the policy, and then sent to the library's management services team (branch managers and higher) for final approval. Some policies may require approval by a library board, a school board, or a city manager. All of this takes time, so be prepared.

The proposal for a policy change should give your decision makers the appropriate background information. Why are you proposing the change? What will the impacts be on staffing? What procedures will need to be changed? Will there be any costs associated with the change? Will signs or informational fliers need to be changed? Will there be any public relations implications? When will the change take effect? Will it require a pilot or roll-out period, or can a date be set for the change?

As a YA librarian, you may not have any actual control over a budget. As noted before, young adult materials are often part of the adult or children's materials budget. You should still find out something about how the budget in your library is developed and administered. Think about the various elements of a library budget: materials, personnel, supplies, and general overhead costs. Any time you propose a program or service, you should have some idea of how it will be paid for. Will money for supplies for the summer reading program come from the Friends of the Library, or is there a budget for crafts and programs? Will you be expected to solicit donations from local businesses to get prizes for your programs? If you want to add a new format like video games to the collection, will the money for that have to come out of some other area of the materials budget?

Again, marshal your facts. Look at library usage statistics and make a case for receiving a larger percentage of the materials budget. Always remember that not all costs are apparent on the surface. If you decide to add a new format, someone in technical services will have to order it, catalog it, process it, and get it ready for the shelves. And what about shelves? Will a new format require a new type of shelving? There's another cost. Your library has resources—people, money, space, collections—but the question is always how they are allocated. To get your fair share for YA, you will need to be aware of what those resources are, what you will need, and where they will come from.

A good way to learn about the budgeting process is to apply for a grant. The Library Services and Technology Act (LSTA) is a federal grant program that is managed by the Institute of Museum and Library Services (IMLS) and administered in the individual states, usually by the state library. IMLS also administers grants directly. Both LSTA and IMLS grants are usually for specific types of projects. Do your research first, and find out if you have a project that fits into the requirements. These are the large grants; there are many smaller grants available from local companies or organizations. Completing a grant application is excellent experience in a whole host of administrative skills. Generally, you need to create a budget and a time line with specific goals, and grants often require that you identify collaborators in the community. Usually grants must be signed by the library director. Large library systems may have their own grant application process that you must follow, and some have a grant writer on staff who must be involved in every grant. The purpose of this is to focus the library's resources on the most likely grants, and to make sure that the library is not creating its own competition for grant funds. So it is essential that you find out what your library expects you to do before you even start the official grant application. You may also have to have the grant application completed a week or more before the final deadline so that your director or review committee has ample time to review it and sign it before it is due. Filling out a grant application is a lot like taking a comprehensive exam or going for a job interview: it is crucial that you answer the questions that are asked, and answer them fully.

Developing physical facilities that support your service goals is another important process. According to Anthony Bernier, "the vast majority of libraries devote more space and design attention to restrooms than to young people." He points out that YA spaces are not just about collections, but rather that "young people should be considered part of the civic community and that libraries should express this value in the designs of their public spaces."[1] In a white paper written for YALSA, Kimberly Bolan says,

> Making libraries appealing and important to teenagers is not an impossible task. Library facilities design is one integral step in attracting teen customers and redefining libraries of the future. Looking at teen facilities design in a new light, letting go of antiquated ideas, re–evaluating traditional ways of doing business, and emphasizing customer needs and wants are essential first steps in moving forward in the world of twenty-first-century libraries.[2]

Today there are many resources for the library that wants to create a teen-friendly space. Some of these resources are noted at the end of this chapter. See the boxed text on pages 48–50 for some ideas on how to start.

It is not enough to be the one person in the library who knows about and practices excellence in service to teens. It can only work if the whole library

As the YA coordinator, I had an in-service for frontline staff on teen spaces with an outside presenter, who is an authority in the field. After the in-service, I arranged for the presenter to speak with the library director for a few minutes. By the end of the meeting, the director had hired the presenter as a consultant to work with the library on teen spaces.

Making the director aware of a leader in the field (outside his own library) made the issue stand out and need action.

Nick Buron
Associate Director
Central Library, Queens (New York) Library

gets on board. As noted in chapter 1, one of the ways you can do this is to keep up with journals and research and share relevant findings with the rest of the staff. Other things you can do include:

- Offer to give a presentation about teen development at an all-staff meeting. People forget what it was like to be a teenager, and all of the staff—including clerks, pages, and security guards—need to be reminded about what is normal teen behavior and how best to deal with it.
- Save up stories about positive interactions with teens and share them at staff meetings, on the staff bulletin board, in e-mail, or on the staff blog.
- Occasionally do a skit or role-playing exercise at a staff meeting: a teen's-eye view of a typical library transaction, for example. Be gentle. You don't want to offend your coworkers, just remind them that teens are people, too.
- Make sure that some of the other staff, not just you, know the names of some of your regulars. Teen librarians know the power of the name; share a little of it with your coworkers.
- Start a young adult book group with staff. Most adults are not aware of the great YA books that are being published these days. Reading a teen novel together can help you discuss issues of teen development and behavior in a nonthreatening way.
- Survey the staff to find out what their greatest issues and concerns are with the teens who use your library. Determine whether there is something you can do to alleviate those concerns or to address

Having a teen space is seen as a vital part of serving teens. But where does that leave libraries that, for whatever reason, can't get the funding? Or what if, no matter how supportive your administration is, they can't enlarge your teen space any more than it is? I am of the opinion that even if funding can't be acquired, we can do simple, cost-effective things to make the teens feel at home in whatever space we have. Here are a few things my library has done in the past few months.

Make a scrapbook of teen photos—take photos of teens at your library doing homework, volunteering, or attending events and put them in an inexpensive photo album. Use whatever scrapbooking skills you have to make it fun. Use a collage style. Put the scrapbook somewhere in your teen section with a sign: "Are YOU in our Hall of Fame?" Teens love looking at pictures. This is a simple way to show teens that this is their library. It's also a great advertising tool and may convince teens who don't attend your program to begin doing so. Total cost: ten dollars or less; save money by printing pictures on regular copy paper.

Put teen art in your teen space or anywhere in your library—call local schools and ask them to consider bringing a class project to your library. Place a sign near the art that says which school and what grades are represented. During your teen advisory board meetings, have teens make small art pieces and place them on your shelves. Total cost: free.

Let teens make the space their own by allowing them to paint the bookends. Bookends can be painted with book themes. Make sure to prime the bookends first.

Find ways to let teens recommend books—teens will read books that other teens suggest. Allow your teen advisory board or book club members to mark their favorites. Give each teen a laminated set of bookmarks that have their name on it. You can also use clothespins with laminated tags on them that you pin to the book.

Lindsey Dunn
Young Adult Librarian
Eva Perry Library, Wake County (North Carolina) Library

those issues. This may give you fodder for future staff meeting topics or for an all-staff e-mail.

- If your library has high school– or college-age pages (shelvers), see if you can get them involved with teen programs.

Once upon a time, there was a teen librarian who wanted more space for her teens . . .

When I started at Oxford Public Library in 1997, I had 180 square feet of space in an alcove designated Young Adult for sixth through twelfth grades. This was a brand new building then. There was shelving on two walls only; the third wall was brick and had a door in it and there was no fourth—it was the opening to the alcove. There were four large square chairs that took up the whole of the center of the room. It was quite claustrophobic. We had about five hundred YA titles in the collection.

I started collecting statistics. It turned out that my collection of books was very popular. I paid attention to what went out and what teens wanted. Teens asked for things; I added them. The circulation stats justified giving me a collection development budget just for teens, separate from youth. As the collection grew, it was only the fact that between 25 and 33 percent of the items were consistently out simultaneously that saved me from being ridiculously overcrowded in that 180 square feet of space.

I work full-time, forty hours a week, and spent my time at the Children's Service Desk, which was across a hallway from the alcove. Teens hated coming into the children's area to get help. They wanted to know why they didn't have a place where they could get help—the little kids and adults had their own service desks; why didn't they? And they weren't happy when I wasn't here; they didn't think that the other staff was able to help them as well as I could. I'm not disparaging my fellow staff; they certainly are competent. It's just that their specialty was more youth-oriented, and not teen.

Of course, as I'm growing the teen collection, the teens are also growing. As they got older, they didn't want to be part of the Youth summer reading program anymore; it was too babyish. So I started doing programming as well, giving teens programs just for them, separate from youth.

As my programming statistics and circulation statistics continued to climb, we had an auspicious thing happen: some space within the library became available for repurposing. We had been leasing two thousand square feet to the Parks and Recreation Department, and they were getting their own building.

So the library surveyed the community to see what they most wanted done with the new space. Overwhelmingly, they asked for more space for teens and more space for computers. The statistics I had collected helped decide how much of that two thousand square feet would become Teen; we ended up with almost half.

In late 2004, I began to work with one of our original architects to decide how we could make a spectacular and functional space for teens. We included teens in focus groups to ask their opinions and ideas. The end result was that in late 2005, we had a beautiful new space, newly designated as Teen Services. At twelve hundred square feet, with seven computers just for teens, a dedicated staff (one full-time and three part-time), and the crown jewel: a service desk just for teens that is staffed all hours the library is open. I believe this is still one of only a few dedicated teen service desks in the state of Michigan.

We now have a ten-thousand-item collection that includes one of the largest graphic novel collections in the state; media in the forms of audio, video, and music; popular and well-attended summer reading programs; and other programming throughout the year.

And the teens and teen librarian lived happily ever after. . . :-)

Charli Osborne
Head of Teen Services
Oxford (Michigan) Public Library

Keep a log of your young adult programs, so you will know what worked and what didn't. Note costs, attendance, reaction, and other input from the teens and from the library community. Not only will this help you in planning future programs and services, but you can use these statistics in defending future requests for funding.

Learning some basic management and administrative skills will enable you to put your YA agenda forward in positive and productive ways. These skills will help you as you grow in your career, and ultimately they will help you serve young adults better.

SUGGESTED READING

Bernier, Anthony. "A Space for Myself to Go: Early Patterns in Small YA Spaces." *Public Libraries* 48, no. 5:33–47.

Bolan, Kimberly. *Teen Spaces: The Step-by-Step Library Makeover,* 2nd ed. Chicago: American Library Association, 2008.

Bolan, Kimberly, for YALSA. "The Need for Teen Spaces in Public Libraries: A White Paper." www.ala.org/ala/mgrps/divs/yalsa/profdev/whitepapers/teenspaces .cfm.

Caplan, Audra. "Defending the YA Budget." *Young Adult Library Services* 8, no. 1:24–25.

Dresang, Eliza, Melissa Gross, and Leslie Edmonds Holt. *Dynamic Youth Services through Outcome-Based Planning and Evaluation.* Chicago: American Library Association, 2006.

Dudden, Rosalind Farnham. *Using Benchmarking, Needs Assessment, Quality Improvement, Outcome Measurement, and Library Standards: A How-to-Do-It Manual with CD-ROM.* New York: Neal-Schuman Publishers, 2007.

Farrelly, Michael. *Make Room for Teens! A Guide to Developing Teen Spaces in the Library.* Westport, CT: Libraries Unlimited, 2009.

Feinberg, Sandra, and James R. Keller. *Designing Space for Children and Teens in Libraries and Public Places.* Chicago: American Library Association, 2010.

Scanlon, Kevin. *New Directions for Library Service to Young Adults.* Chicago: American Library Association, forthcoming.

Suellentrop, Tricia. "It's Not about You." *School Library Journal* 54, no. 4:27.

Vaillancourt, Renee J. *Managing Young Adult Services: A Self-Help Manual.* New York: Neal-Schuman Publishers, 2002.

"YA Spaces of Your Dreams" column. *Voice of Youth Advocates.*

Zilonis, Mary Frances, Carolyn Markuson, and Mary Beth Finkle. *Strategic Planning for School Library Media Centers.* Lanham, MD: Scarecrow Press, 2002.

NOTES

1. Anthony Bernier, "A Space for Myself to Go: Early Patterns in Small YA Spaces," *Public Libraries* 48, no. 5:33–47.
2. Kimberly Bolan, for YALSA, "The Need for Teen Spaces in Public Libraries: A White Paper." www.ala.org/ala/mgrps/divs/yalsa/profdev/whitepapers/teenspaces.cfm.

chapter FIVE

COMPETENCY AREA V
Knowledge of Materials

THE LIBRARIAN will be able to:

1. Meet the informational and recreational needs of young adults through the development of an appropriate collection for all types of readers and nonreaders.

2. Develop a collection development policy that supports and reflects the needs and interests of young adults and is consistent with the parent institution's mission and policies.

3. Demonstrate a knowledge and appreciation of literature for and by young adults in traditional and emerging formats.

4. Develop a collection of materials from a broad range of selection sources, and for a variety of reading skill levels, that encompasses all appropriate formats, including, but not limited to, media that reflect varied and emerging technologies, and materials in languages other than English.

5. Serve as a knowledgeable resource to schools in the community as well as for parents and caregivers on materials for young adults.

Santa Clara County (California) Library

Philosophy of the Teen Collection

Materials in the teen collection of the Santa Clara County Library are selected to reflect the current recreational and informational needs of thirteen- to eighteen-year-olds or those in junior and senior high. A wide range of subjects and formats comprise the collection because of the vast differences in the emotional, social, and intellectual development, as well as the diverse interests of the target group.

The teen collection focuses on recreational and personal growth, rather than curriculum support. Most of the titles are written either specifically for the age group or are selected from the adult collection because of their appeal to teens. All reading and interest levels of the targeted age group are spanned. Recognizing that teen needs are varied and changing, it is still possible to identify certain topics which will always be of interest to teens: the search for self-identity, the separation from family, adjustment to sexuality, conflict with the older generation, the development of personal goals and values, and humor. Materials in the teen collection address these interests as well as offering information on current culture and information literacy.

The task in reviewing for the teen collection is to select, while keeping the above interests in mind, materials that may be of interest to teens and will have an emotional or intellectual impact.

The overall goal is to keep teens reading and in the library.

The teen collection should be displayed for high browsing appeal and be regularly weeded.

Teen collections include:

- An attractive display of new materials (published in the last six to twelve months)
- Fiction books arranged by author with hardbacks, mass market, and trade paperbacks interfiled
- Nonfiction books on teen life issues and personal growth
- Graphic novels
- Console games
- Magazines
- Pamphlets selected by teen librarians
- Booklists produced by Santa Clara County Library and other reputable organizations

Teen collections may include:

- Anime
- Talking books
- Classics, Cliffs Notes
- DVDs
- Reference copies of local textbooks

Teen collections do not include:

- Rock CDs that are selected for all ages
- Curriculum support materials, with the exception of items mentioned above; these are purchased and interfiled in the adult collection

It is almost a guarantee that the young adult librarian will know far more about young adult materials than anyone else in the library. It is therefore important for the YA librarian to hone that knowledge, share it with others in the library, and know how it fits into the larger picture of the library's collection.

Start by reading carefully your institution's collection development policies and procedures. Are young adult materials mentioned at all? If not, are there places that YA materials should be mentioned? Do the policies and procedures support excellent young adult service? Young adults have different needs than children and than adults. Find out if those differences are addressed in the policy. Teens' developmental needs and the range of intellectual and emotional growth in the teen age range should be considered in selecting materials specifically for teens.

Next, create a separate YA collection development policy that fits in with the larger institution's policy. For example, if your library has made the policy decision that it only collects popular materials—best sellers, genre fiction, feature film DVDs, popular music CDs, and so on—then your YA collection will most likely follow that strategy as well. The issue of whether or not to collect curriculum-related materials may be one that the library has discussed and made a decision about. It may collect only popular nonfiction in the children's area, but not make an attempt to purchase everything that supports the curriculum at local schools. At the Santa Clara County Library (see boxed text on page 54), "the teen collection focuses on recreational and personal growth, rather than curriculum support." Teen Services provides "nonfiction books on teen life issues and personal growth" but not curriculum support materials, with the exception of classic literature and Cliffs Notes. The adult and children's departments at these libraries collect broadly and deeply in many areas that can and do serve as curriculum support. But these items are not shelved in the teen area.

At the Haverhill (Massachusetts) Public Library, "non-fiction titles should provide a balance between popular, high interest titles and those that supplement the curriculum of the Haverhill Public Schools." (See boxed text below.) Haverhill shelves most teen nonfiction with adult nonfiction, with the exception of what they call the "self-help" collection, which includes "titles published for teenagers with an aim of improving their lives or handling situations they may encounter."

At the Morton Grove (Illinois) Public Library, "the Young Adult collection is comprised of fiction titles and graphic novels selected specifically to meet the recreational needs of teens." (See boxed text, pages 58–59.) The adult nonfiction collection at this library is intended to serve "residents over the age of twelve," and nonfiction materials for teens are considered part of the adult collection.

To meet the need for popular materials in a teen collection, it may be reasonable to collect console games, anime, manga and graphic novels, and other formats that the adult and children's departments do not normally

From the Haverhill Public Library Collection Development Policy

The Teen Services Department is intended to serve Haverhill youths from sixth through twelfth grades as well as their parents/caregivers and teachers. The community has a diverse background in terms of race, faith, sexual preference, and ethnicity, which shall be reflected within the Teen Services collection.

The Teen Services collection includes fiction (in hardcover, trade paperback, and mass market paperback formats), graphic novels (including traditional graphic novels in paperback or hardcover and manga), magazines, audio materials (available in a variety of media to stay current with technological trends), video games, and nonfiction materials which are shelved within the adult collection (with the exception of a teen self-help collection).

Haverhill (Massachusetts) Public Library
www.haverhillpl.org/About/policies/teenmaterials.html.

collect. Collections will vary from library to library, as the collection plans shown here illustrate, but the key is to make sure that your library is clear about what the teen collection consists of. The policies shown here are merely examples; yours will vary according to your own library's larger collection policies and the decisions you and your administration make about the teen collection.

Selection sources for young adult materials may also differ from those in the adult and children's departments. Sources that include information about the various formats (games, anime, etc.) are critical, as well as those that review young adult materials specifically. Being aware of emerging technologies and formats is essential for the young adult librarian. Monitoring blogs, professional journals, and electronic discussion lists will help you to keep up. You should also consider sources for items in languages other than English and items at varying reading levels. You may need to subscribe to some additional selection sources, beyond what the library normally uses. Be sure you know what selection sources are already available in your library. If they contain reviews of YA materials, ask to be on the routing list.

To demonstrate a knowledge and appreciation of literature for and by young adults, it is necessary to read. Read reviews in journals, read review blogs, read books, read the booktalks of others. Read widely in all sorts of genres. Take advantage of all the great resources and expertise YALSA offers. In a YALSA white paper entitled "The Value of Young Adult Literature," Michael Cart states that YALSA "values young adult literature, believes it is an indispensable part of public and school library collections, and regards it as essential to healthy youth development and the corollary development of healthy communities in which both youth and libraries can thrive."[1]

YALSA's Booklists and Book Awards website (www.ala.org/yalsa/booklists) is the single best starting place for learning about young adult literature. For more than fifty years, YALSA members have spent thousands of hours creating booklists of the best books for teens, and YALSA has created several awards to honor the best in young adult literature each year. These booklists and awards are decided every year by committees of YALSA members who read widely, attend ALA Annual and Midwinter conferences, and debate the merits of individual books and media items.

YALSA booklist deliberations are open to the membership and the general public. Field nominations are encouraged, as is attendance at committee meetings. At committee meetings, members of the audience are given an opportunity to share their opinions of the nominated titles. Through 2010, both ALA Annual and Midwinter conferences, one Best Books for Young Adults committee session has been set aside for teens to comment on the nominated books.

Morton Grove (Illinois) Public Library

The Young Adult collection is comprised of fiction titles and graphic novels selected specifically to meet the recreational needs of teens. The fiction collection consists primarily of young adult novels and genre literature covering mystery, science fiction, fantasy, and romance. Since circulation tends to be greater among paperback titles for this age group, the library emphasizes the paperback format over hardcover editions.

Graphic novels are selected from the same fiction genre listed above, as well as from nonfiction works of interest to teens.

Influencing Factors
The problems, adventures, and topics of interest confronting teens on a daily basis are the factors to consider when selecting titles.

Selection Plan
The tools of selection for young adult fiction include *Booklist, Kirkus Children and Young Adult Reviews, VOYA, Ingram Paperback Advance,* and *School Library Journal.* Publishers' catalogs, such as those from Bantam, Dell, Random House, and Fawcett, are also used. Occasionally, titles by outstanding young adult authors, major book award winners, or other titles deemed by the Young Adult selectors to have lasting interest for teens will be purchased in hardcover editions. Remaining titles selected from the review journals listed above are held in reserve until the paperback editions are available. *Kliatt* is used as a selection tool specifically for young adult paperback titles.

In addition to the sources listed above for young adult fiction, selection tools for graphic novels include *Library Journal, Publishers Weekly,* and titles displayed in local bookstores.

Retention and Weeding
Due to space limitations and circulation statistics, only popular, circulating titles should be retained. Weeding should be continual and titles should be replaced by new materials of current need and interest. Sources such as *Senior High School Catalog, Best Books for Young Adults,* and other reliable sources may be checked before a specific title is withdrawn.

Development Plan
Paperback and graphic novel displays and the further development of the graphic novel collection should continue to be an integral part of this collection

with new paperback titles replacing older and less read hardcover titles. Popular series titles will continue to be included in the Young Adult collection. The value of the Young Adult collection as a separate entity should be periodically re-evaluated and a plan developed to optimize space and materials reserved for this collection.

———
Morton Grove (Illinois) Public Library
www.webrary.org/inside/colldevadultya.html.

This practice will continue on the Best Fiction for Young Adults Committee. YALSA award deliberations, on the other hand, are confidential. All committee meetings are closed to the membership and the general public, although nominations from the membership are welcome. The committee has discretion about whether to include a field-nominated title in their deliberations.

BOOKLISTS

Best Books for Young Adults (BBYA). Annotated lists going back to 1998 can be found on YALSA's website. Each list contains from sixty to eighty fiction and nonfiction books that cover the whole range of interests of teens from twelve through eighteen years old. BBYA members read hundreds of books each year, debate them passionately, and gather input from teens. Books selected are chosen on the basis of both quality and popularity. Each year, the committee also chooses their Top Ten list from among the year's books. These generally are the books that were overwhelmingly popular with both committee members and teens. Not every book on BBYA will appeal to every teen, but the lists are good starting places. For information about older Best Books, see *Best Books for Young Adults*, 3rd ed., edited by Holly Koelling for YALSA. YALSA also periodically offers an ALA pre–conference and pulls together a Best of the Best list. The latest version was completed in 2005, and a pamphlet that includes annotations and brief bibliographic information is available from ALA. After the publication of the 2010 list, Best Books for Young Adults evolved into the Best Fiction for Young Adults booklist.

Best Fiction for Young Adults (BFYA). Beginning in 2011, this list will honor outstanding fiction titles that are of interest and value to teenagers. In addition to the full list, the committee will select a Top Ten from among the year's fiction books. Field nominations are encouraged, and the committee

Baltimore County (Maryland) Public Library

Teen Nonfiction Collection Description

This collection contains books primarily published for teens ages twelve through eighteen. This is not a comprehensive collection but rather focuses on nonfiction titles of particular interest to adolescents. Curricular material is not purchased for this browsing collection; books for this age level with assignment-related content are purchased for the Juvenile or Adult collections. Instead, this area contains high-interest titles covering a wide range of subjects.

All Dewey areas are included in this relatively small section of the collection as a whole. In most branches, a new Teen Nonfiction section highlights the recent material to the collection, before these items are inter-shelved with the rest of nonfiction.

In addition to the general criteria outlined above, specific attention is paid to:

1. subject relevance and age appropriateness of material

2. precision and accuracy of coverage

3. competence of writing style

4. clarity in the organization of material

5. quality of illustrations, maps, graphics, and photographs

6. artistic merit of work

7. usefulness of material for homework assignments

8. popularity of subject

General Purchasing

Teen nonfiction is published in both hardcover and paperback binding and usually varies in price, ranging from $5.99 to $30.00. Titles are not purchased in library binding.

Most titles are bought widely, and titles with higher interest levels and print runs are purchased with some duplication for branches with the highest circulation. Teen nonfiction also lends itself to in-branch browsing, which is considered when selecting the material. Branches with nearby middle or high schools may receive additional titles or copies in the initial purchase distribution.

Replacement Purchasing

New and updated titles will always be purchased for the subjects contained in this collection. Specific title replacement is limited as older material that contains outdated information will not be reconsidered for replacement. Teens are acutely aware of when material becomes outdated and/or outmoded.

Exceptions to this replacement model include:

- Award-winning titles which remain popular
- State and regional local interest
- Informational or recreational titles addressing subjects which are static in content

Subject Purchasing

Selection within the teen nonfiction category includes, but is not limited to, the following subjects:

100s   *Chicken Soup* titles, self-help, dealing with friends, parents, siblings

200s   Religious works, especially Christian-themed teen titles

300s   Sociological commentaries, such as materials about racial and GLBT issues

300s   Preparing for college or post–high school life

600s   Dating, sex, puberty, pregnancy, health, diet, and exercise

600s   Beauty and grooming, hair and makeup

700s   Photography and art by or for teens

700s   Games and sports books written for teens, especially extreme sports and skateboarding, etc.

800s   Collections of essays, humor, quotations, poems by or for teens; biographies written specifically for teens

will hear opinions from teens at ALA's Midwinter Meeting and Annual Conference.

Quick Picks for Reluctant Young Adult Readers. This list is for teens (ages twelve through eighteen) who, for whatever reason, do not like to read. It is not intended for remedial or curricular use, but rather to create a list of

Johnson County (Kansas) Library

Young Adult Collection Development Policy

Young adult materials are selected for upper elementary grades through early high school levels, with the major emphasis placed on the middle school or junior high level. Young adult collections are designed to complement the recreational reading, listening, and viewing materials available at Johnson County Library. Materials in the young adult nonfiction collection concern topics of interest to young people, with a focus on personal, social, and emotional needs.

www.jocolibrary.org/templates/JCL_InfoPage.aspx?id=2061.

recreational reading that will grab nonreaders. Lists going back to 1996 are available on the website. Lists include both fiction and nonfiction, and the books are evaluated by subject, cover art, readability, format, style, and teen feedback. Teen feedback is especially critical for this list, as it is intended to be a list of books that reluctant readers would self-select. Field nominations are encouraged, as are audience comments at the committee meetings.

Popular Paperbacks for Young Adults (PPYA). PPYA is actually a series of several lists each year. The committee first decides how many lists (from one to five) it will create, and then selects the genres, topics, or themes to be considered. For example, the 2009 PPYA lists were on the topics of "Bodies," "Change Your World," "Hard Knock Life," and "Twists on the Tale." The committee then seeks from ten to twenty-five books on each topic. Titles chosen must be in print and available in paperback, may be either fiction or nonfiction, and may be published for either adults or young adults. In selecting the titles, popularity is more important than literary quality. Lists going back to 1997 are available on the website. PPYA is an excellent resource for themed booklists and displays, and for readers' advisory based on topic.

Outstanding Books for the College Bound. This list is revised and updated every five years. Its intent is to provide reading recommendations for people of all ages who want to continue their education beyond high school. Its primary audience is students in grades nine through twelve who wish to enrich and strengthen their knowledge of various subject areas in both classic and contemporary literature. The list can be used to recommend reading for high school students studying for college entrance examinations. It is also an

Manske Library, Farmers Branch (Texas)

The standard selection tools used to select titles for [Young Adult Fiction and Young Adult Nonfiction] include: *School Library Journal, Hornbook, The Bulletin of the Center for Children's Books, VOYA, Children's Catalog,* and *Booklist.* Reviews from one or more of these sources are usually consulted before a title is purchased. In addition, bibliographies such as *A to Zoo, Best Books for Children, Best Books for Junior High Readers, The Book Finder,* and *Children's Books in Print* are used to select specific titles on desired subjects. School reading lists and subject lists from professional library journals are also consulted for titles for possible purchase.

Books are purchased to fill patron requests when possible. The review sources and bibliographies mentioned above are consulted to ensure the suitability and availability of the requested titles.

www.farmersbranch.info/play/manske-library/code-conduct-policies/collection-development.

excellent list for anyone of any age who simply wants to round out his or her knowledge of literature, both fiction and nonfiction, in the areas covered by the list. Categories vary slightly from edition to edition, but the 2009 version included Arts and Humanities, History and Cultures, Literature and Language Arts, Science and Technology, and Social Sciences. Both young adult and adult books are considered. A compilation of earlier lists can be found in *More Outstanding Books for the College Bound, 2005 Edition.*

Great Graphic Novels for Teens. This list began in 2007, in response to teens' growing interest in the graphic novel format. An annotated list of recently published graphic novels appropriate for teens is prepared each year. Titles include both fiction and nonfiction, published for both adults and young adults.

Amazing Audiobooks for Young Adults (formerly Selected Audiobooks for Young Adults). This list began in 1999, and each year presents a selection of notable audio recordings appropriate for and appealing to young adults ages twelve through eighteen. The committee looks for a professional quality production that may include, among other things, effective use of voices, music, sound effects, and language, appropriateness of material for audio presentation, suitability of match between performer and text, and possible expansion of audience of young adults for a text that has not been readily accessible in its print format to its target audience. Annotated versions of all of the lists are available on the website.

Fabulous Films for Young Adults. This list underwent a major overhaul in 2008, with 2009 marking the first list in the new format. Prior to this time, Selected DVDs and Videos for Young Adults was a list of films under sixty minutes, produced in the two preceding years, and of interest to teens. The new Fabulous Films list is meant to identify for collection developers a body of films relating to a theme that will appeal to young adults in a variety of settings. The Fabulous Films list in 2009 used the theme "Coming of Age around the World" and includes sixteen films, both feature (*Juno, Bend It Like Beckham, 10 Things I Hate about You*) and non-feature (*Dogtown and Z-Boys, Devil's Playground, Persepolis*) that deal with what it's like to come of age in different places and diverse cultures. This list, along with Amazing Audiobooks and Great Graphic Novels, reflects YALSA's belief that access to library collections that reflect young adult interests and needs is essential and that multimedia formats are necessary to accommodate varied interests.

Teens' Top Ten. This is a "teen choice" list, first offered in 2003, where teens nominate and choose their favorite books of the previous year. Nominators are members of teen book groups in fifteen selected school and public libraries around the country. Nominations are posted on Support Teen Literature Day during National Library Week, and teens across the country vote on their favorite titles each year. Winners are announced during Teen Read Week. This is a list of recent books, nominated by teens who have read widely in the available literature, and voted on by teens. Consider using this list with teens who are "social readers" and who like to read what their friends are reading.

AWARDS

Alex Awards. This award is given annually, since 1998, to ten books from the previous year written for adults that have special appeal to young adults (ages twelve through eighteen). Nonfiction and fiction in various genres are included in the list. This list acknowledges the fact that many teens read books that were published for adults. Many, in fact, go directly from reading children's literature to reading adult literature. The committee attempts to narrow the large field of adult books by selecting ten that are well written, readable, and potentially appealing to teens. Beginning in 2010, the Alex Award committee publishes its official, vetted nomination list on the YALSA website.

The William C. Morris YA Debut Award. This award was first given in 2009. It celebrates the achievement of a previously unpublished author, or authors, who have made a strong literary debut in writing for young adult readers. An estimated three thousand YA titles are published annually, and an informal survey of publishing staff indicated that approximately 10 percent of the titles on their lists were debuts. This award was established to recognize those debut authors, to encourage authors to write for young adults, and to highlight achievement by previously unpublished authors. In a departure from the procedures for other committees, the William C. Morris Award committee announces a short list of up to five titles in early December. This allows members an opportunity to read these titles before the award announcement at the ALA Midwinter Meeting.

YALSA Award for Excellence in Nonfiction for Young Adults. Offered for the first time in 2010, this award recognizes the best in nonfiction books for teens. As with the Morris Award, a short list of up to five titles is announced in early December, with the award being presented at the ALA Midwinter Meeting. A complete list of official nominations is published on the YALSA website after the Youth Media Awards in January.

Odyssey Award. This award was first presented in 2008. Jointly chosen by YALSA and the Association for Library Service to Children, it honors the producer of the best audiobook for children and/or young adults. One winner and multiple honor titles may be selected. The titles may cover the entire range of children's and young adult literature, from birth to age eighteen. Not all titles will appeal to all ages.

Margaret A. Edwards Award. Although this is sometimes known as a "lifetime achievement" award, it honors not only an author, but a specific body of his or her work for significant and lasting contribution to young adult literature. It recognizes an author's work in helping adolescents become aware of themselves and addressing questions about their role and importance in relationships, society, and in the world. The award has been given annually since 1988 to an author whose book or books, over a period of time, have been accepted by young adults as an authentic voice that continues to illuminate their experiences and emotions, giving insight into their lives.

Books cited in the award must have been published for at least five years, allowing them time to reach a wide level of distribution and be accepted by young adults. The list of winners is a veritable "Who's Who" of young adult literature, and every young adult librarian ought to be aware of all of these authors and at least some of their work.

Michael L. Printz Award. The Printz Award honors a book from the previous year that exemplifies literary excellence in young adult literature. One award and up to four honor titles are selected. This award is based solely on literary excellence. Although appeal to the intended audience (teens) can be considered a factor in determining quality, popularity among teen readers is not considered specifically in presenting the award. The award was first presented in 2000. While fiction has dominated the list of winners and honor books, nonfiction, poetry, and graphic novels have also been included, and the fiction has included fantasy, science fiction, historical fiction, and realistic fiction.

OTHER RESOURCES

Other resources include YALSA's Ultimate Teen Bookshelf, available as a PDF download, which highlights must-have teen materials for libraries. The fifty books, five magazines, and five audiobooks on the Bookshelf list were suggested by members of the YALSA-BK electronic discussion list and vetted by two experienced YA librarians, Pam Spencer Holley and Judy Sasges.

The YALSA wiki contains dozens of themed booklists compiled by YALSA members and by members of the YALSA-BK discussion list. YALSA-BK itself can be a good source of titles for readers' advisory if you are stuck, but it is always worthwhile to check the wiki first to see if someone has already created the list you're interested in.

Be sure you involve your teens when it comes time to decide what to buy for your young adult collection, and even what to weed. If you have a teen advisory group, or even just a group of regular library users, they can tell you which series are up-and-coming and which are passé. Find out what magazines they read and what television shows they watch; that will also help you know what the next big thing is likely to be in your collection. Generally speaking, young adult book collections should be a good mix of literary fiction and nonfiction for teens and the more ephemeral popular works that teens want right now.

Creating finding aids will help the teens in your community find their favorite series as well as the kinds of information they may need for school projects. Especially if curriculum-related nonfiction is not shelved in your

As librarians, we are all familiar with the importance of reading reviews in professional journals, as well as online blogs related to YA fiction. However, in order to stay aware of what the teens in the community you serve are reading, it is necessary to talk to those teens. When I see teens browsing for books, I ask them if I can help them pick out something new to read. Not only do I get to help them and make a connection with those teens, but I also get the chance to hear from them about the titles they have recently read and enjoyed. I also often hear comments like, "Oh, my friend read that and she really liked it," or "My cousin said that one has a bad ending because the main character dies and she thought the story would turn out better." When teens check out books at our desk, I encourage them to come back to tell me how they like the book. Many of them never do, but some teens come back again and again for recommendations and to talk about the books they really enjoyed. Teens sometimes recommend books I would never have picked up on my own and this expands my knowledge of teen fiction.

———

Michele Gorman
Teen Services Coordinator
Charlotte Mecklenburg (North Carolina) Library

teen area, you will need to make it easy for the teens to find their way to the adult nonfiction section where those things may be found. See chapter 6 for more on making collections accessible.

Lists of all types in various formats (printed bookmarks, online lists, displays) will not only help your teens find items they are interested in, they will help other staff members find materials for teens. In many libraries, the young adult librarian is there only some of the hours the library is open. If you are the only one who knows anything about YA literature, you will want to make it easy for your colleagues to help teens. Having lists they can refer to is one way to accomplish this. Another way is to introduce the literature to the rest of the staff.

Booktalking is not only for teens. Ask if you can have five minutes (or more) out of each staff meeting to booktalk one or two YA books that the rest of the staff may never have heard of. Or start a book discussion group at your library among the library staff. Include clerks and pages as well as supervisors, and children's and adult librarians. Meet over lunch, before work, after work, or whenever you can find a half hour that a few people can gather. Most people who work in libraries are book people at heart. If you get such a program started, you will undoubtedly find others who want to participate and share books with you.

Meanwhile, don't forget that there is more to YA materials than books. Magazines are extremely popular with many teens, especially boys. Browse the magazine sections at local bookstores, hobby stores, music stores, and video game stores to find out what is out there and what your teens might enjoy. Again, ask the teens what they are interested in and find magazines in those subject areas. Audiobooks, videos, and video games are other formats that teens are interested in. Research review sources for these items, and be alert to suggestions from teens.

Teens are often unaware of the rich variety of electronic resources that libraries have available: databases, e-books, downloadable audio and video, and so on. Look at your library's collection of these items from the point of view of teens, and find ways to merchandize them. Take advantage of vendor training to learn how to use your library's databases, and then share that information with teens. These can often be some of the most helpful resources for school assignments.

YALSA has discussion lists and interest groups that can be of use for collection development. There is an anime discussion group, for example, whose purpose is to "discuss issues relating to anime and to develop and disseminate best practices in collections, programming, and related topics in the popularity of anime and its effects on teens. Regularly share good program practices and successful anime events as well as making anime title recommendations to the group." There is also a music interest group, "to develop recommended practices in collections, programming, and related topics in the field of music and media, including CDs, MP3s, and emerging technologies and services in music media for teens."[2] Information about interest groups and discussion groups and how to join one or start one can be found on YALSA's website.

Reading and nonreading teens are users of the library. Understanding their needs, having a collection policy that reflects those needs, and having a knowledge and appreciation of literature for young adults is one major way that libraries serve teens. As the only (or one of the few) people in the library with the responsibility to serve teens, knowledge of YA materials and how to develop a YA collection is likely to fall squarely on you. Fortunately, there are plenty of resources to help you.

SUGGESTED READING

Aronson, Marc. *Exploding the Myths: The Truth about Teenagers and Reading.* Lanham, MD: Scarecrow Press, 2001.

Bartel, Julie, and Pamela Spencer Holley. *YALSA Annotated Book Lists for Every Teen Reader: The Best from the Experts at YALSA.* New York: Neal-Schuman Publishers, 2010.

Bodart, Joni Richards. *Radical Reads 2: Working with the Newest Edgy Titles for Teens.* Lanham, MD: Scarecrow Press, 2009.

Booth, Heather. "RA for YA: Tailoring the Readers Advisory Interview to the Needs of Young Adult Patrons." *Public Libraries* 44, no. 1:33–36.

Booth, Heather. *Serving Teens through Readers' Advisory.* Chicago: American Library Association, 2007.

Brenner, Robin E. *Understanding Manga and Anime.* Westport, CT: Libraries Unlimited, 2007.

Cart, Michael, for YALSA. "The Value of Young Adult Literature: A White Paper." www.ala.org/ala/mgrps/divs/yalsa/profdev/whitepapers/yalit.cfm.

Creel, Stacy L. "Early Adolescents' Reading Habits." *Young Adult Library Services* 5, no. 4:46–49.

Frouland, Tina, for YALSA. *The Official YALSA Awards Guidebook.* New York: Neal-Schuman Publishers, 2008.

Goldsmith, Francisca. *The Readers' Advisory Guide to Graphic Novels.* Chicago: American Library Association, 2010.

Gorman, Michele. "An Extreme Makeover." *School Library Journal* 54, no. 8:21.

Gorman, Michele. "Step Up to the Plate: Teens and Controversial Materials." *School Library Journal* 53, no. 6:31.

Halsall, Jane, and R. William Edminister. *Visual Media for Teens: Creating and Using a Teen-Centered Film Collection.* Westport, CT: Libraries Unlimited, 2009.

Herald, Diana Tixier. *Teen Genreflecting: A Guide to Reading Interests.* Westport, CT: Libraries Unlimited, 2003.

Holley, Pamela Spencer, for YALSA. *Quick and Popular Reads for Teens.* Chicago: American Library Association, 2009.

Howard, Vivian. "Peer Influences on Young Teen Readers: An Emerging Taxonomy." *Young Adult Library Services* 8, no. 2:34–41.

Hubert, Jennifer. *Reading Rants: A Guide to Books That Rock!* Westport, CT: Libraries Unlimited, 2007.

Jones, Patrick, Maureen L. Hartman, and Patricia Taylor. *Connecting with Reluctant Teen Readers: Tips, Titles, and Tools.* New York: Neal-Schuman Publishers, 2006.

Kerby, Mona. *Collection Development for the School Library Media Program: A Beginner's Guide.* Chicago: American Association of School Librarians, 2006.

Koelling, Holly, ed., for YALSA. *Best Books for Young Adults,* 3rd ed. Chicago: American Library Association, 2007.

Mahood, Kristine. *Booktalking with Teens.* Westport, CT: Libraries Unlimited, 2010.

Sullivan, Michael. *Serving Boys through Readers' Advisory.* Chicago: American Library Association, 2010.

YALSA. The Ultimate Teen Bookshelf. www.ala.org/yalsa/handouts/.

NOTES

1. Michael Cart, for YALSA, "The Value of Young Adult Literature: A White Paper." www
.ala.org/ala/mgrps/divs/yalsa/profdev/whitepapers/yalit.cfm.
2. YALSA Discussion and Interest Groups. www.ala.org/ala/mgrps/divs/yalsa/about
yalsab/discussion.cfm.

chapter SIX

COMPETENCY AREA VI
Access to Information

THE LIBRARIAN will be able to:

1. Organize physical and virtual collections to maximize easy, equitable, and independent access to information by young adults.

2. Utilize current merchandising and promotional techniques to attract and invite young adults to use the collection.

3. Provide access to specialized information (i.e., community resources, work by local youth, etc.).

4. Formally and informally instruct young adults in basic research skills, including how to find, evaluate, and use information effectively.

5. Be an active partner in the development and implementation of technology and electronic resources to ensure young adults' access to knowledge and information.

6. Maintain awareness of ongoing technological advances and how they can improve access to information for young adults.

One of the jobs of the teenager is to become independent, and it is the job of the YA librarian to facilitate that growth. This can be done by making physical and virtual YA collections and spaces easy to access. How to achieve that will differ from library to library, but the principles are the same everywhere.

First, think about the physical YA collection in your library. Are YA items housed in a separate YA area or are they interfiled with adult or children's materials? If there is a separate YA section, is it near the children's area, the adult area, or someplace entirely separate? Are all materials classified as YA housed in that same area, or are some collections (music or videos, for example) shelved somewhere else? Any of these options can work, but the real question is, when a teen walks into your library, how will he or she know where to go to find what is wanted?

Look at your library as if you were walking into it for the first time. One good way to do this is to give someone a tour of the library, as if that person is going to come and work there and needs to know where everything is. If you find yourself constantly explaining why something is in one place or another, it is a good clue that your organization may not be entirely intuitive. Another way is to swap libraries with a colleague: you walk through her library and she walks through yours, then you give each other notes on what you saw. Ask the teens who use your library how they use it and how they find what they need.

What you have shelved in your YA collection will depend on your library's collection development policy and philosophy of YA services. (See chapter 5.) One of the ongoing debates among YA librarians is what to do with YA nonfiction. First, what does the YA nonfiction collection consist of? Is it only popular, high-interest material, or are curriculum support materials included? If curriculum support materials are not shelved with the other YA materials, but rather interfiled with adult materials, are teens aware of how to find them when they need them? If they are shelved with the other YA materials, is it clear to teens that they may need to look in more than one place to find materials for their school reports and projects?

Mary Anne Nichols writes:

> Typically teens do not ask for suggestions from library staff when looking for materials. A YALSA-sponsored program on teens and research skills at the 2000 ALA Annual Conference in Chicago reinforces this statement. A panel of teenagers present at the program admitted that they want help in finding information but rarely turn to a librarian to ask for it. When asked why, one teen responded, "I think it is a bit of pride. Teenagers think it's like being a little kid to go and ask a librarian."[1]

Here's one of my favorite projects, called Teen Picks.

1. A sign encourages teens to fill out a small (roughly three-by-five-inch) card that asks for the title, author, and brief review of a favorite book. Cards are put into a ballot-style box.

2. I (or one of my volunteers) empty out the box periodically, and input the information into a Microsoft Word template I designed, listing only first names for privacy purposes, but otherwise trying to keep intact everything the teen wrote. If a teen just lists a book, I generally paste in a description of the book from the catalog. I keep a small index box of these printed-out cards.

3. The picks themselves are located on the same shelving unit as the ballot box. It's a small, double-sided shelf, with slat-wall shelving on its narrow sides. I use a variety of wire and plastic displayers, and generally fit about twenty books on the unit. I tape the teen reviews to the bottom of the displayer. Periodically (usually about once a week), I replace the empty displayers with new books and reviews, keeping the old cards so I have plenty to check through next week (since many of the books teens choose are popular, and thus not available for display, I usually can only just fill up the shelf, although that is changing as my index box fills up).

It is also a wonderful tool for collection development. Basically every week I get a review of a book that either is lost from our branch or we never owned. I am constantly purchasing books based on these recommendations, both for our branch out of my replacement funds, and for the whole system out of my paperback funds.

The next step for me is to get it tied into our online presence. I already have the reviews in electronic format, so it would be relatively easy to get those loaded up onto one of our sites, if there were an appropriate place for it. This might happen with the teen site redesign I'm working on.

I've been really surprised at how well it has worked out. I get new reviews constantly (I have to weed out a few snarky ones, but generally they take it seriously), and I estimate that at least half of the twenty books displayed are gone by the time I refill the next week. I refilled yesterday evening, and this morning three were gone already.

Mark Flowers
YA Librarian
JFK Library, Solano County Library system
Vallejo, California

If the teens are not going to come to us, we must reach out to them, with clear signage, attractive displays, and useful finding aids.

There are some relatively simple things you can do to make the collection more accessible to teens. Take a look at your collection. Is it visually appealing to teens? Most YA book covers are colorful and interesting; the more of them that you can shelve face-out, the better they will be seen and the more likely they will move. Is there room to browse? In his book *Why We Buy,* Paco Underhill talks about the "butt brush effect": Browsers "don't like being brushed or touched from behind. They'll even move away from merchandise they're interested in to avoid it."[2] Do you have display shelving? Look through some catalogs for ideas of different types of display shelving. Some can be incorporated into your existing shelving, like slat-wall units for the end panels or slanted shelves in place of flat.

If you are going to pull items out of the regular collection and put them on display shelving, you will need to make sure that the rest of the staff knows where these items are. Other reference staff, shelvers, and those whose job it is to search for requests will all need to know where to find items. Use the capabilities of your ILS to change the status of items on display. Keep staff informed of what you are doing, and get them on board by showing them the positive results of your merchandising efforts.

Think about signs. Signs are useful, but you do need to be careful with them. A few well-designed signs can help, but our tendency as librarians is to over-sign things, to the point where no one reads them. Paco Underhill says, "So you can't just look around your store, see where there are empty spots on the walls and put the signs there." Unfortunately, that is often the library approach. Underhill notes that "putting a sign that requires twelve seconds to read in a place where customers spend four seconds is just slightly more effective than putting it in your garage."[3] Do some research and create effective signs that look professional and are long-lasting. Get your teens to help.

Labeling can be useful, but it is wise to be careful with it. Labeling materials by age or grade might seem like a good way to match teens with books, but it can also turn off teens who don't want to be seen reading a book below their grade level. Before labeling, be sure to read ALA's "Labeling and Rating Systems: An Interpretation of the Library Bill of Rights" (appendix F) and "Questions and Answers on Labels and Rating Systems" (appendix G). The interpretation states,

> While knowing the reading level of a book can assist library users, organizing a library via these labels can pose a psychological barrier for users who do not know their reading level.

Many will feel that they should not utilize those resources. Users who do know their reading level may feel compelled to only select resources from their reading level. This will result in users not utilizing the full scope of the library collection.[4]

The same principles of organizing your physical space apply to your virtual space. Find out if your local teens are aware of your web presence. Make your teen website interesting and accessible. As with signs, avoid being overly wordy. Spend some time looking at the teen web pages of other libraries and look for ideas to make your own site look clean, useful, and teen-friendly. Keep it up to date and change the content often, in order to keep the teens coming back. Create a plan for updating your web presence, and make it part of your daily or weekly tasks.

As discussed in chapter 4, sometimes library policies can prevent teens from having full access to information in the library. Time limits on computer usage, mandatory blocking software, and limiting teens to computers in certain areas of the library can all have a dampening effect on their ability to find the information they want and need. It is the job of the YA librarian to minimize those deterrents by advocating for teens and their needs.

Most teens, as noted above, don't want to ask for help, even when they acknowledge that they need it. One way to make them independent library users is to provide instruction on how they can use the library to meet their own needs. Formal instruction can take place in a variety of ways. School librarians can teach about the resources in the school library. Public librarians can arrange to go to schools and share information about the public library's resources. Classes can visit the public library. Public librarians can also use their community contacts to present programs at other places that teens gather, like a recreation center or after-school homework center.

If you are a public librarian, talk to your local school librarian(s) and find out what kind of library instruction is happening in the schools. The level of instruction that is available in schools varies widely from district to district and state to state. In California, for example, many districts are lucky to have one librarian for all of the elementary schools and one for the middle and high schools. In those cases, very little library instruction is going on in the schools, and more falls onto the public librarians. Also, don't forget that there are probably private schools in your service area, and homeschooled students as well. Some private schools, especially high schools, have strong school libraries and dedicated librarians; others rely heavily on the public library. Find out what the situation is in your area, and how you can collaborate in either case. Homeschoolers will probably approach you, but find out if there is one or more homeschooling associations in your area and make contact. They are usually delighted to have your help.

Once you have determined what type of library instruction for teens is happening in the schools, you can plan what types of instruction to do in and outside of the library. In collaboration with the school library, decide whether it would be more effective to plan visits to schools to instruct students directly, or to arrange for presentations to teachers so that they can share the information with their students. In a recent article, Donna Gilton notes that "some public libraries have created information literacy instruction and other outreach activities, specifically to reach public school teachers." She cites the Providence (Rhode Island) Public Library and the Multnomah County (Oregon) Public Library as examples of libraries that have extensive programs aimed at teachers, including professional collections, book discussions, workshops, bulk loans, and many other services.[5]

If you are a school librarian, you should find out what resources your public library has to offer. Often the public library, especially if it is part of a large system or consortium, can afford more extensive database collections than the school district can. Public libraries frequently offer programs, such as author visits, lectures, and cultural programs, which can support the curriculum. Giving students credit or another incentive to attend these public library events can benefit the school by supplementing the curriculum, and the public library by getting more teens in the door and exposing them to the kinds of things the library has to offer.

Teens may think they know everything there is to know about the library, but they usually don't. Many librarians have experienced the situation in which they surveyed teens or had a suggestion box, and discovered that many of the items, programs, and services that teens are asking for are already being supplied. Start thinking about ways you can spread the word to teens about what is available in the library. Technology can be your friend.

In recent years, a few libraries have started moving away from the dependence on the Dewey decimal system and trying bookstore-type classification schemes. This is one of those decisions that you are not going to be able to make on your own, but it is worth reading up on the subject and finding out what some of the possibilities are. Proponents of both Dewey and non–Dewey classification schemes insist that their method makes it easier to find items. "Findability is complicated," says Michael Casey. "To some it means locating things easily while browsing and to others it means finding things precisely after doing a catalog search."[6] Both groups must be considered. Many of the libraries that are "de-Deweying" as well as those that aren't are experimenting with new types of shelf signs that make it easier for browsers to find the sections they are looking for. When the Redwood City Public Library in California opened its new Redwood Shores branch in 2009, they shelved in Dewey order, but created large, easy-to-read signs for the top of each range of shelving indicating the subject matter. The 800s, for example, were labeled "Poetry, Plays, and Essays." In the children's area, the 900s were labeled "History, Geography, Explorers." Take a look at your YA area and consider ways that you can make materials, especially nonfiction, easier to find and less intimidating.

One big way you can improve access and increase circulation is to weed. Getting rid of the old, tattered, out-of-date materials makes the good stuff shine. Dated cover art can spell doom for the best book. Publishers sometimes release old favorites in new covers, so watch for these, and replace your old versions. Make weeding a regular part of your routine. This is another place you can engage other members of the staff. You can encourage the staff who check in materials and those who shelve them to bring you items that are falling apart, ugly, or torn. Use your library's ILS to give you reports on what has not been checked out, and get rid of those. Reports like this will also help you find the items that are missing from the collection. These should almost always be replaced; if someone stole it, it is probably good, or at least important to someone. Failing to replace stolen items on the basis that they will just get stolen again is really just another way of restricting access to materials.

Access to information also involves coping with challenges to materials, including the Internet. At some point it is likely that someone, probably a parent, will challenge a book, video, game, or other item in your YA collection. To avoid being caught off guard, find out what systems your library has in place to deal with challenges. Read your library's policy manual, and have copies of "Request for Reconsideration" forms, if they exist. Find out what the chain of command is for challenges to materials. ALA's Office of Intellectual Freedom (OIF) is a great resource for challenges, but don't wait until a challenge hits before you go to the website and read their materials. The OIF staff is prepared to help you deal with challenges. They have strategies and tips for dealing with the media, for talking to concerned parents or other patrons one-on-one, and give some examples of key messages. Here are the OIF's tips for children's and young adult librarians coping with challenges:

- Make sure you and your staff are familiar with the library's collection policy and can explain it in a clear, easily understandable way.
- Take time to listen to and empathize with a parent's concern. Explain in a nondefensive way the need to protect

the right of all parents to determine their own children's reading.

- Keep your director informed of any concerns expressed, whether you feel they have been successfully resolved or not.
- Join professional organizations to keep abreast of issues and trends in library service to children and families.
- Encourage parents or guardians to participate in choosing library materials for their young people and to make reading aloud a family activity. Host storytelling, book discussion groups, and other activities that involve adults and youth.
- Offer "parent education" programs/workshops throughout the year. National Library Week in April, Teen Read Week in October, and Children's Book Week in November provide timely opportunities. Suggested topics: how to select books and other materials for youth; how to raise a reader; how books and other materials can help children and teens cope with troubling situations; the importance of parents being involved in their children's reading and library use; concepts of intellectual freedom.
- Reach out to the media. Offer to write a newspaper column or host a radio or TV program discussing good books and other materials for children and teens. Give tips for helping families get the most from libraries.
- Build bridges. Offer to speak to parent and other groups on what's new at the library, good reading for youth, how to motivate children and teens to read, how to make effective use of the library, and other topics of special interest.[7]

The YALSA office will also be glad to help you deal with challenges.

Access to information expresses almost everything we do as librarians. As a YA librarian, your focus should always be on providing the best possible access for teens. As you look at all of your programs, services, and collections, consider the question of access, and how you can improve it and make it more equitable for teens, enabling them to find the information they need and want.

SUGGESTED READING ————————————————————————————

Adams, Suellen S. "Marketing the Homework Center Digitally." *Young Adult Library Services* 8, no. 2:11–12.

American Association of School Librarians. *Information Power: Partnerships for Learning.* Chicago: American Library Association, 1998.

American Association of School Librarians. *School Library Media Programs in Action: Civic Engagement, Social Justice, and Equity.* Chicago: AASL, 2009.

ALA Office of Intellectual Freedom. "Censorship in the Schools." www.ala.org/ala/aboutala/offices/oif/ifissues/censorshipschools.cfm.

ALA Office of Intellectual Freedom. "Challenge Support." www.ala.org/ala/issuesadvocacy/banned/challengeslibrarymaterials/copingwithchallenges/index.cfm.

ALA Office of Intellectual Freedom. "Intellectual Freedom Manual." www.ala.org/ala/aboutala/offices/oif/iftoolkits/ifmanual/intellectual.cfm.

Carlson, Chris, and Ellen Brosnahan. *Guiding Students into Information Literacy: Strategies for Teachers and Teacher-Librarians.* Lanham, MD: Scarecrow Press, 2009.

Chelton, Mary K., and Colleen Cool, eds. *Youth Information-Seeking Behavior: Theories, Models, and Issues.* Lanham, MD: Scarecrow Press, 2004.

Chelton, Mary K., and Colleen Cool, eds. *Youth Information-Seeking Behavior II: Context, Theories, Models, and Issues.* Lanham, MD: Scarecrow Press, 2006.

Doyle, Miranda. *101+ Great Ideas for Teen Library Websites.* New York: Neal-Schuman Publishers, 2007.

Fister, Barbara. "The Dewey Dilemma." *Library Journal* 134, no. 16:22–25.

Gilton, Donna L. "Information Literacy as a Department Store: Applications for Public Teen Librarians." *Young Adult Library Services* 6, no. 2:39–44.

Gorman, Michele, and Tricia Suellentrop. *Connecting Young Adults and Libraries: A How-To-Do-It Manual,* 4th ed. New York: Neal-Schuman Publishers, 2009.

Grassian, Esther S., and Joan R. Kaplowitz. *Information Literacy Instruction: Theory and Practice,* 2nd ed. New York: Neal-Schuman Publishers, 2009.

Nichols, Mary Anne. *Merchandising Library Materials to Young Adults.* Westport, CT: Libraries Unlimited, 2002.

Peowski, Laura. "Where Are All the Teens: Engaging and Empowering Them Online." *Young Adult Library Services* 8, no. 2:26–28.

Underhill, Paco. *Why We Buy: The Science of Shopping.* New York: Simon and Schuster, 1999.

YALSA and RUSA. *Guidelines for Library Services to Teens, Ages 12-18.* Chicago: ALA, 2008. http://yalsa.ala.org/guidelines/referenceguidelines.pdf.

NOTES

1. Mary Anne Nichols, *Merchandising Library Materials to Young Adults* (Westport, CT: Libraries Unlimited, 2002), 28.
2. Paco Underhill, *Why We Buy: The Science of Shopping* (New York: Simon and Schuster, 1999), 18.
3. Ibid., 63.
4. ALA, "Questions and Answers on Labels and Rating Systems." www.ala.org/ala/issues advocacy/librarybill/interpretations/faq-labeling.cfm.
5. Donna L. Gilton, "Information Literacy as a Department Store: Applications for Public Teen Librarians," *Young Adult Library Services* 6, no. 2:41.
6. Michael Casey and Michael Stephens, "It's Fine to Drop Dewey," *Library Journal* 134, no. 12:19.
7. ALA, "Tips for Children's and Young Adult Librarians." www.ala.org/ala/issues advocacy/banned/challengeslibrarymaterials/copingwithchallenges/strategiestips/index.cfm#tipschildrenyoung.

chapter SEVEN

COMPETENCY AREA VII
Services

THE LIBRARIAN will be able to:

1. Design, implement, and evaluate programs and services within the framework of the library's strategic plan and based on the developmental needs of young adults and the public assets libraries represent, with young adult involvement whenever possible.

2. Identify and plan services with young adults in nontraditional settings, such as hospitals, homeschool settings, alternative education, foster care programs, and detention facilities.

3. Provide a variety of informational and recreational services to meet the diverse needs and interests of young adults and to direct their own personal growth and development.

4. Continually identify trends and pop-culture interests of young people to inform and direct their recreational collection and programming needs.

5. Instruct young adults in basic information gathering, research skills, and information literacy skills—including those necessary to

evaluate and use electronic information sources—to develop lifelong learning habits.

6. Actively involve young adults in planning and implementing services and programs for their age group through advisory boards, task forces, and by less formal means (i.e., surveys, one-on-one discussion, focus groups, etc.).

7. Create an environment that embraces the flexible and changing nature of young adults' entertainment, technological, and informational needs.

The key to providing programs and services for teens is to follow the same ideas we have been exploring throughout this book: consider the library's mission and strategic plan, the YA mission and plan, and the developmental needs of teens, and involve teens in planning and implementing the programs and services. Not all "services" for teens are programs. Services include all the various ways libraries serve teens: collections, reference, readers' advisory, the library's online presence, the physical building and the teen space(s) within it, and outreach services to schools and other places where teens may be found. Programs may be ongoing, like book clubs and volunteer programs; they may be onetime, like author events and gaming tournaments; or they may last for several days or weeks at a time, like summer reading programs, Teen Tech Week, or Teen Read Week.

In a study presented in *Public Libraries* in 2007, Denise Agosto of Drexel College of Information Science and Technology surveyed teens in public libraries in Pennsylvania and New Jersey and asked them, "Why did you come to the library today?" She found that teen library use fell into three major categories: Library as Information Gateway, including information for personal needs and for schoolwork; Library as Social Interaction/Entertainment Space, including interaction with peers and with library staff, and organized as well as unorganized entertainment; and Library as Beneficial Physical Environment, including refuge, personal improvement, and community improvement (volunteering).[1] These findings support the research on positive youth development and developmental assets that we have been using throughout this book.

There are many guides and resources for teen programming, but they are not "one size fits all." Every teen librarian has had the experience of planning for a big program, advertising it to teens, preparing the library staff, and then having two or three or even no teens show up. As with all other programs and services, the best way to get the teens there is to involve them in the

Studio i is Charlotte Mecklenburg Library's (CML's) Blue Screen Animation and Music Production Studio, located on the second floor of ImaginOn in the Loft, CML's teen-only library. In an effort to engage teens in the process of making policies and procedures for the studio, in 2009 teens were invited to bring any questions or concerns about current policies, along with ideas about new ways to encourage patrons to know, understand, and follow guidelines. The hopes were that by incorporating teens in the process, they would feel more ownership in the space and therefore be more likely to respect the rules agreed upon. It was also important to get feedback on the consequences for refusal to follow the policies so that teens would feel the entire process was fair to all users. The current rules and regulations for the studio are very teen-friendly, goal-oriented, and a solid reflection of the teens who use that creative space every day.

Michele Gorman
Teen Services Coordinator
Charlotte Mecklenburg (North Carolina) Library

planning process. Find out what kinds of programs your teens want, and get them invested in planning and organizing them. They will then see to it that their friends show up.

Reference services to teens pose a unique challenge. Teens are not children; they are developing critical thinking skills, their reading ability is much the same as that of many adults, and they are developing the ability to hypothesize. They are also not yet adults. They are extremely self-conscious and they become easily embarrassed. They are often reluctant to ask for help, but when they do, "teens approach the reference desk with two main types of questions: the 'imposed' query (usually a school assignment) and the personal query (often a popular culture interest)."[2] The imposed query can be particularly difficult for the reference librarian, because often the teen does not fully understand what the assignment is, and, more important, doesn't really care. But the personal query is often even more difficult, especially if the librarian is not familiar with current trends and popular culture interests.

Consider ways in which you can make the reference transaction easier, both for the teens and for yourself and other library staff. Are there ways you can anticipate the school assignments, and have materials ready to share? If you have made contacts at local schools, as discussed in chapter 3, you will have a source for finding out what the upcoming assignments are.

- Be alert to new assignments as the teens approach you. If you can find a teen who actually has a written copy of the assignment, make a photocopy and keep it at the reference desk.
- Keep an assignment binder and write down the best resources you have found. Add to it as you learn others.
- During the summer, make a list of hot topics that are likely to come up during the school year. Science fairs, literary criticism and author biographies, and U.S. history are perennial favorites. List online and print sources that are appropriate for these topics.
- Create paper and online pathfinders with a few good sources for common assignments.
- Be aware of the current year's national debate topics (www.nfl online.org/StudentResources/Topics).
- Be sure all staff members who work at the adult and children's reference desks are aware of your binders, pathfinders, and other resources.

Readers' advisory is another major service that libraries can offer teens, but it can also be a challenge. Teens often want help finding something to read, but are reluctant to ask a librarian. There are numerous resources on readers' advisory for teens, but there is no real substitute for reading the materials that the teens like. Heather Booth points out that "unless teens have interactions to show that librarians can provide a variety of leisure reading options, specifically for their particular interests, our suggestions, just like school assignments, may be viewed as work rather than fun."[3]

- Make a list for yourself of some ways you can identify trends and current pop-culture interests.
- Identify two or three magazines that you can read regularly to help you keep up with the latest celebrities.
- Identify some websites that will help you do the same thing. Add them to your RSS feed aggregator.
- Listen when the teens talk. If necessary, make a note for yourself to look up the topics or people being discussed.

Your library's website is one way that teens will gain access to the library. It should have a separate YA space that focuses on the particular needs and interests of teens. Spend some time looking at the YA pages of several libraries. Include libraries that are about the same size and demographics as yours, as well as some of the better-known and better-funded libraries. Look at

Library Journal's "Star Libraries" and the top libraries in Hennen's American Public Library Ratings (www.haplr-index.com). Check out their websites and see what they are doing for their teen pages.

A website can be a good way to get information to teens that they are reluctant to ask for, so be sure to include links and information about drugs, sexuality, health, and other social issues. Include phone numbers for hotlines (suicide prevention, drug abuse, etc.) and links to referral and information sites (eating disorders, crisis pregnancy, etc.). Use your contacts with other youth-serving organizations to make sure you are aware of everything your community has to offer.

Identifying and planning services with young adults in nontraditional settings involves first finding out who and where these teens are. The needs assessment process you undertook in chapter 4 should help you with finding this information, as should the contacts with other youth-serving organizations you made in chapter 3. A 2008 article in *Public Libraries* on library service in juvenile detention centers showed a wide range of services offered to this particular group, from an in-house branch of the public library with full services to bookmobile or other book delivery service. Booktalks, discussion groups, author visits, and writing workshops were some of the other services offered in some detention facilities.[4] These are likely the same kinds of programs and services you are offering in the library. Consider which you could offer in nontraditional settings. Set some goals for increasing service to these groups over the next six months, one year, and two years. As discussed in chapter 4, you will need to create a plan and a justification, and include information on the cost of such a project, including personnel costs.

Social networking offers another option for serving teens who are not necessarily in the library. In 2006, YALSA bloggers posted ideas every day for a month about how social networking could be used by teens in positive ways. Connecting specific online tools with the principles of positive youth development, YA librarians talked about ways in which they were using social networking tools in their programs and services in public and school libraries. These blog posts were saved on YALSA's website and are a good starting place for ideas on how to gear new services to the needs of the community. Highlights included ways that social networking can be used to:

- Empower teens
- Give teens the chance to meaningfully serve the community
- Support teen reading and writing/text-based literacy needs and skills

- Give teens opportunities to create and collaborate
- Make sure teens are able to plan and manage projects
- Communicate with community members
- Provide teens with opportunities to choose how to be smart and safe when using technology.[5]

In recent years, gaming has emerged as a significant library service, especially for teens. Julie Scordato of the Columbus (Ohio) Metropolitan Library notes,

> The first thing to recognize about American video game culture is that it's not a niche consumer group and hasn't been for a very long time. Playing video and computer games is a normal part of teens' daily media consumption and, in the case of online games, media creation.[6]

She adds, "By providing video game programs to teens, you have an opportunity to build an incredible amount of teen participation in, and identification with, the library." Game programs often include board and card games as well. A list of resources for gaming in the library can be found at Infopeople's website at http://infopeople.org/resources/gaming.

Booktalking has long been a staple of YA services. A number of the resources listed at the end of this chapter will give you information on the basics of booktalking. Check out YALSA's resources on booktalking at www.ala.org/ala/yalsa/profdev/booktalking.htm. Bear in mind that there are many different ways to booktalk. If it is difficult for you to schedule time in the schools for booktalking, look for other places you can do it. Concentrate on short "grabbers" that you can share with teens as you are talking with them in the library. As noted in earlier chapters, you can also use your booktalking skill to share teen books with other library staff, with parents, and with community partners. You can booktalk online, using your library's blog or social networking site. Work with your teen advisory group or book discussion group on booktalking tips so they can share books with their friends. Encourage them to share booktalks online, if possible, or offer them a place to share information about their favorite books in the library. (See the "Teen Picks" example on page 73.) Consider gathering lists of good new titles or themed resource lists to send out to teachers or counselors or your community partners once or twice a year, or before special events.

Knowing teens and their interests enables you to create more ways for them to participate. Youth participation in library groups meets several of

A few years ago I worked with the Southeast Massachusetts Regional Library System (SEMLS) on an IMLS project. The project was to develop a website for teens that could act as a one-stop shop for locating information and connecting with each other. The development of the site happened just before the MySpace/Facebook boom and was before lots of the current Web 2.0 technologies were available. That said, the SEMLS administration realized that libraries in their area were not effective in supporting teens via the Web and didn't have the skills to develop websites and web content that met teen technology and informational needs; hence, the grant.

As a part of the project team I worked with teens to develop ideas for the site. Teens were involved in helping to select the Web development firm that was hired to work on the back end and the front end of the site. A few teens sat in on informational meetings with web developers and asked questions of the developers in order to get a sense of how well the professionals would be able to work with the age group. The teens helped to determine what content would be on the site and participated in online chats where they provided information on how they use technology and what they would like to see in a website of this kind from a library. Teens helped come up with the name for the site and also worked to decide what the site would look like. Once the site launched, teens were involved in ongoing maintenance as well as moderated discussion boards on the site.

Linda W. Braun
Educational Technology Consultant
LEO: Librarians and Educators Online

the external developmental assets and gives teens an opportunity to develop some of the internal assets, as discussed in chapter 2. Talk to teens at your library, identify an area of interest, and design a club that focuses on that. Book discussion groups are an obvious example, but there may be something else that is more to the liking of your teens. Consider options like a graphic novel group, an anime group, a writing group, a classic film group, a craft group, or a gaming group. Gather a group of interested teens and, along with them, make some decisions about when and how often the group will meet, how meetings will be organized, and so on. Will your book discussion group all read the same book and discuss it, or will it be more of a book-sharing group, where everyone talks about what they have been reading? Are there ways to involve others who don't actually attend the meetings? Perhaps your group members can write reviews that are posted to a library blog or even on a physical bulletin board. They could create book trailers for posting on YouTube or podcasts about their favorite books.

We all know that teens have much to offer in our schools and communities. By creating programs and services that utilize and showcase the talents and skills of local young adults, libraries give the whole community an opportunity to see teens in a different light.

SUGGESTED READING

Agosto, Denise. "Why Do Teens Use Libraries? Results of a Public Library Use Study." *Public Libraries* 46, no. 3:55–62.

Alessio, Amy, and Kimberly A. Patton. *A Year of Programs for Teens.* Chicago: American Library Association, 2006.

Booth, Heather. "RA for YA: Tailoring the Readers Advisory Interview to the Needs of Young Adult Patrons." *Public Libraries* 44, no. 1:33–36.

Booth, Heather. *Serving Teens through Readers' Advisory.* Chicago: ALA Editions, 2007.

Braun, Linda W. *Teens, Technology, and Literacy: Or, Why Bad Grammar Isn't Always Bad.* Westport, CT: Libraries Unlimited, 2007.

Coleman, Tina, and Peggie Llanes. *The Hipster Librarian's Guide to Teen Craft Projects.* Chicago: American Library Association, 2008.

Czarnecki, Kelly. "Dream It, Do It: At the Library! Technology Outreach at a Juvenile Detention Center." *Young Adult Library Services* 7, no. 2:22–24.

Doyle, Miranda. *101+ Great Ideas for Teen Library Websites.* New York: Neal-Schuman Publishers, 2007.

Farmer, Lesley. *Teen Girls and Technology: What's the Problem, What's the Solution?* Chicago: American Library Association, 2008.

Gallaway, Beth. *Game On! Gaming at the Library.* New York: Neal-Schuman Publishers, 2009.

Gilman, Isaac. "Beyond Books: Restorative Librarianship in Juvenile Detention Centers." *Public Libraries* 47, no. 1:59–66.

Gorman, Michele, and Tricia Suellentrop. *Connecting Young Adults and Libraries: A How-To-Do-It Manual,* 4th ed. New York: Neal-Schuman Publishers, 2009.

Honnold, RoseMary. *More Teen Programs That Work.* New York: Neal-Schuman Publishers, 2005.

Honnold, RoseMary, for YALSA. *Get Connected: Tech Programs for Teens.* New York: Neal-Schuman Publishers, 2007.

Infopeople. "Resources on Gaming in Libraries." http://infopeople.org/resources/gaming.

Jones, Ella W. *Start-to-Finish YA Programs: Hip-Hop Symposiums, Summer Reading Programs, Virtual Tours, Poetry Slams, Teen Advisory Boards, Term Paper Clinics, and More!* New York: Neal-Schuman Publishers, 2009.

Jones, Patrick, Maureen L. Hartman, and Patricia Taylor. *Connecting with Reluctant Teen Readers: Tips, Titles, and Tools.* New York: Neal-Schuman Publishers, 2006.

Kan, Katherine, for YALSA. *Sizzling Summer Reading Programs for Young Adults,* 2nd ed. Chicago: American Library Association, 2006.

King, Kevin. "Get with the Program" column. *Voice of Youth Advocates.*

Levine, Jenny. *Gaming and Libraries: Learning Lessons from the Intersections.* Chicago: ALA Tech Source, 2009.

Lillian, Jenine, for YALSA. *Cool Teen Programs for Under $100.* Chicago: YALSA, 2009.

Mahood, Kristine. *Booktalking with Teens.* Westport, CT: Libraries Unlimited, 2010.

McLellan, Kathy, and Tricia Suellentrop. "Serving Teens Doing Time." *Voice of Youth Advocates* 30, no. 5:403–7.

Neiburger, Eli. *Gamers—in the Library?! The Why, What, and How of Videogame Tournaments for All Ages.* Chicago: American Library Association, 2007.

Nicholson, Scott. *The Role of Gaming in Libraries: Taking the Pulse.* http://board gameswithscott.com/pulse2007.pdf.

Osborne, Charli. "Crafting Cheap and Successful Teen Programs." *Young Adult Library Services* 8, no. 1:15–17.

Ott, Valerie. *Teen Programs with a Punch: A Month-by-Month Guide.* New York: Neal-Schuman Publishers, 2006.

Rockefeller, Elsworth. "Striving to Serve Diverse Youth: Mainstreaming Teens with Special Needs through Public Library Programming." *Public Libraries* 47, no. 1:50–55.

Saricks, Joyce. *Readers' Advisory Service in the Public Library,* 3rd ed. Chicago: American Library Association, 2005.

Scordato, Julie. "Gaming as a Library Service." *Public Libraries* 47, no. 1:67–73.

Snow, Jessica. "Library Outreach to Foster Teens." *Young Adult Library Services* 8, no. 1:20–23.

Spielberger, Julie, Carol Horton, Lisa Michels, and Robert Halpern. *New on the Shelf: Teens in the Library—Findings from the Evaluation of Public Libraries as Partners in Youth Development.* www.chapinhall.org/research/report/new-shelf.

Suellentrop, Tricia. "Get Out of the Library!" *School Library Journal* 52, no. 9:39.

Sullivan, Michael. *Serving Boys through Readers' Advisory.* Chicago: American Library Association, 2010.

YALSA and RUSA. *Guidelines for Library Services to Teens, Ages 12–18.* http://yalsa. ala.org/guidelines/referenceguidelines.pdf.

NOTES

1. Denise Agosto, "Why Do Teens Use Libraries? Results of a Public Library Use Study," *Public Libraries* 46, no. 3:58.
2. YALSA and RUSA, *Guidelines for Library Services to Teens, Ages 12–18*. http://yalsa.ala .org/guidelines/referenceguidelines.pdf.
3. Heather Booth, "RA for YA: Tailoring the Readers Advisory Interview to the Needs of Young Adult Patrons," *Public Libraries* 44, no. 1:33.
4. Isaac Gilman, "Beyond Books: Restorative Librarianship in Juvenile Detention Centers," *Public Libraries* 47, no. 1:64.
5. YALSA, "Teens and Social Networking in School and Public Libraries." www.ala.org/ ala/mgrps/divs/yalsa/profdev/socialnetworkingtool.pdf.
6. Julie Scordato, "Gaming as a Library Service," *Public Libraries* 47, no. 1:67–69.

chapter EIGHT

STARTING FROM SCRATCH

WHAT IF your library does not have a teen services department, or librarian, or budget? How can you use the competencies to get yourself to where you want to be? No matter where you are, there are almost certainly teens in your service area. If they are part of your service area, your library should be serving them.

You are already reading this book, which is a good place to start. Look at some of the resources listed at the end of each chapter. Join YALSA and look at all of the resources that YALSA has to offer. Decide, based on your current situation, whether your greatest need is to create a separate teen space in the library to house teen collections and activities; to create a separate teen librarian position; or to create a separate teen services budget line for materials, programs, or both. Understand how your library works. What is its organizational structure and how is it funded? What is the budget and how is it divided?

Look at the information on collecting statistics in chapters 1 and 4. Gather data on current YA usage of your library, and develop methods to track YA usage in areas where they don't already exist. Look at what teens are checking out as well as the circulation of YA materials. Observe how teens are using the library. Are they checking out materials? Are they using the library as a place to hang out? If not, where do they hang out? Are they using the library's computers? As described in chapter 4, do a community analysis and needs assessment, and create a YA services mission and plan.

Analyze the current YA collection. Look at the information in chapter 2 and make sure your knowledge of teens and teen developmental needs is up to date. Be aware of all the teens in your community. Then look at the information in chapter 5 about creating a YA collection development policy. If there has not been any systematic care taken of the YA collection, you will undoubtedly need to start by weeding and refreshing the collection. Make a plan for improving the collection. Identify funding sources for new materials. Bear in mind that these do not have to be new sources. If you can make the case that teen patrons are a significant portion of your service area and that teen materials are a significant portion of your library's circulation, you can lobby for transfer of funds from other areas within the library.

Write a job description for a YA librarian. You don't need to start from scratch. Use the existing job descriptions in your organization and follow that format. Go through the competencies and make notes of specific skills from each of the areas. Be aware, however, that a job description should allow some room for growth. If you simply include all of the competencies as the requirements for a basic-level job, you will find it difficult to hire anyone. The competencies are something that a librarian must grow into over the course of a career.

Create a YA advisory group. This could flow naturally out of your community analysis. A focus group that you create for your needs assessment could become the basis of your teen advisory group. Read chapter 1 for more details on the benefits of teen advisory groups and see the suggested resources for starting a group. Read chapter 3 for information on making connections in the community and on how to advocate for teens. Your community partners and your local teens can be some of your biggest assets in lobbying for more and better service to teens in the library.

Make a plan for your YA space. Look at some of the resources mentioned in chapter 4 for tips on how to carve a YA space out of an existing library. Make the case, as you did with YA collections, for the amount of space teens should have. Describe your ideal YA space, but also make a list of practical things that can be achieved in the next six months, one year, or two years. Again, identify funding sources, if necessary.

Make a YA service plan. Using the library's strategic plan and mission and what you have learned about the developmental needs of teens, list the services that you would like to offer teens in your library. Prioritize the list, based on what you can reasonably accomplish given staffing, funds, and time.

Meet with your library's director. Ideally, you should be meeting with the director on a regular basis, and have his or her backing for a project of this size. However, if there really is no YA department, collection, space, or staff, you may want to do some preliminary research before your first meeting on this topic. At the very least, have some facts and figures at your fingertips. Look at the PLDS survey data (see chapter 1) and read YALSA's white papers on the benefits of dedicated YA staff, literature, and spaces. Look up the census data for your service area, and know how many teens you could potentially serve.

As you develop a plan and bring it to your director, present yourself professionally and calmly, but firmly. Put yourself in the director's shoes and imagine what he or she will want to hear. What benefits will a teen program provide to the library or to the community? How will this fit into what the library is already doing? How much will it cost? Who will do the work? How will the director be able to present the case to the library board or city council?

Young adults deserve the best. That is the core ideology behind the *Competencies for Librarians Serving Youth,* and behind this book. If every library took the competencies seriously and every teen-serving librarian fully attained all of the competencies, libraries and communities would look very much like the future envisioned in the YALSA strategic plan:

- Every public library and every secondary school library would have a qualified YA librarian.
- Every member of the library staff would regard teens as essential and valued library customers.
- Every library would have an equitable budget line item for teen collections and services.
- Every library would have an appropriate and inviting space for teen services.
- All teens would be library users and advocates.
- All teens would be aware of the library as an innovative informational resource.
- Teens would be recognized as a core population served by public libraries.
- Teens would feel recognized as an important constituent within the library and the community.

- Teens would contribute to their own personal development as partners in the planning, creation, and evaluation of library services.
- Communities would recognize YA librarians and school library media specialists as informational experts on serving teens.
- YA librarians and school library media specialists would be actively engaged in the larger youth-serving community.
- YA librarians and school library media specialists would be viewed as advocates for teens in the community.
- YA librarians and school library media specialists would make meaningful contributions to the library profession.

LIBRARY BILL OF RIGHTS

THE AMERICAN Library Association affirms that all libraries are forums for information and ideas, and that the following basic policies should guide their services.

I. Books and other library resources should be provided for the interest, information, and enlightenment of all people of the community the library serves. Materials should not be excluded because of the origin, background, or views of those contributing to their creation.

II. Libraries should provide materials and information presenting all points of view on current and historical issues. Materials should not be proscribed or removed because of partisan or doctrinal disapproval.

III. Libraries should challenge censorship in the fulfillment of their responsibility to provide information and enlightenment.

IV. Libraries should cooperate with all persons and groups concerned with resisting abridgment of free expression and free access to ideas.

V. A person's right to use a library should not be denied or abridged because of origin, age, background, or views.

VI. Libraries which make exhibit spaces and meeting rooms available to the public they serve should make such facilities available on an equitable basis, regardless of the beliefs or affiliations of individuals or groups requesting their use.

Adopted June 19, 1939, by the ALA Council; amended October 14, 1944; June 18, 1948; February 2, 1961; June 27, 1967; January 23, 1980; inclusion of "age" reaffirmed January 23, 1996.

A history of the Library Bill of Rights is found in the latest edition of the *Intellectual Freedom Manual.*

FREE ACCESS TO LIBRARIES FOR MINORS
An Interpretation of the Library Bill of Rights

LIBRARY POLICIES and procedures that effectively deny minors equal and equitable access to all library resources and services available to other users violate the Library Bill of Rights. The American Library Association opposes all attempts to restrict access to library services, materials, and facilities based on the age of library users.

Article V of the Library Bill of Rights states, "A person's right to use a library should not be denied or abridged because of origin, age, background, or views." The "right to use a library" includes free access to, and unrestricted use of, all the services, materials, and facilities the library has to offer. Every restriction on access to, and use of, library resources, based solely on the chronological age, educational level, literacy skills, or legal emancipation of users violates Article V.

Libraries are charged with the mission of providing services and developing resources to meet the diverse information needs and interests of the communities they serve. Services, materials, and facilities that fulfill the needs and interests of library users at different stages in their personal development are a necessary part of library resources. The needs and interests of each library user, and resources appropriate to meet those needs and interests, must be determined on an individual basis. Librarians cannot predict what resources will best fulfill the needs and interests of any individual user based on a single criterion such as chronological age, educational level, literacy skills, or legal emancipation. Equitable access to all library resources and services shall not be abridged through restrictive scheduling or use policies.

Libraries should not limit the selection and development of library resources simply because minors will have access to them. Institutional self-censorship diminishes the credibility of the library in the community, and restricts access for all library users.

Children and young adults unquestionably possess First Amendment rights, including the right to receive information through the library in print, nonprint, or digital format. Constitutionally protected speech cannot be suppressed solely to protect children or young adults from ideas or images a legislative body believes to be unsuitable for them.[1] Librarians and library governing bodies should not resort to age restrictions in an effort to avoid actual or anticipated objections, because only a court of law can determine whether material is not constitutionally protected.

The mission, goals, and objectives of libraries cannot authorize librarians or library governing bodies to assume, abrogate, or overrule the rights and responsibilities of parents and guardians. As "Libraries: An American Value" states, "We affirm the responsibility and the right of all parents and guardians to guide their own children's use of the library and its resources and services." Librarians and library governing bodies cannot assume the role of parents or the functions of parental authority in the private relationship between parent and child. Librarians and governing bodies should maintain that only parents and guardians have the right and the responsibility to determine their children's—and only their children's—access to library resources. Parents and guardians who do not want their children to have access to specific library services, materials, or facilities should so advise their children.

Lack of access to information can be harmful to minors. Librarians and library governing bodies have a public and professional obligation to ensure that all members of the community they serve have free, equal, and equitable access to the entire range of library resources regardless of content, approach, format, or amount of detail. This principle of library service applies equally to all users, minors as well as adults. Librarians and library governing bodies must uphold this principle in order to provide adequate and effective service to minors.

See also "Access to Resources and Services in the School Library Media Program" and "Access for Children and Young Adults to Nonprint Materials."

---

1. See Erznoznik v. City of Jacksonville, 422 U.S. 205 (1975). "Speech that is neither obscene as to youths nor subject to some other legitimate proscription cannot be suppressed solely to protect the young from ideas or images that a legislative body thinks unsuitable for them. In most circumstances, the values protected by the First Amendment are no less applicable when government seeks to control the flow of information to minors." See also Tinker v. Des Moines School Dist., 393 U.S. 503 (1969); West Virginia Bd. of Ed. v. Barnette, 319 U.S. 624 (1943); AAMA v. Kendrick, 244 F.3d 572 (7th Cir. 2001).

Adopted June 30, 1972, by the ALA Council; amended July 1, 1981; July 3, 1991; June 30, 2004; July 2, 2008.

ACCESS FOR CHILDREN AND YOUNG ADULTS TO NONPRINT MATERIALS

An Interpretation of the Library Bill of Rights

LIBRARY COLLECTIONS of nonprint materials raise a number of intellectual freedom issues, especially regarding minors. Article V of the Library Bill of Rights states, "A person's right to use a library should not be denied or abridged because of origin, age, background, or views."

The American Library Association's principles protect minors' access to sound, images, data, games, software, and other content in all formats such as tapes, CDs, DVDs, music CDs, computer games, software, databases, and other emerging technologies. ALA's "Free Access to Libraries for Minors: An Interpretation of the Library Bill of Rights" states:

> The "right to use a library" includes free access to, and unrestricted use of, all the services, materials, and facilities the library has to offer. Every restriction on access to, and use of, library resources, based solely on the chronological age, educational level, literacy skills, or legal emancipation of users violates Article V.
>
> ... [P]arents—and only parents—have the right and responsibility to restrict access of their children—and only their children—to library resources. Parents who do not want their children to have access to certain library services, materials, or facilities should so advise their children. Librarians and library governing bodies cannot assume the role of parents or the functions of parental authority in the private relationship between parent and child.

Lack of access to information can be harmful to minors. Librarians and library governing bodies have a public and professional obligation to ensure that all members of the community they serve have free, equal, and equitable access to the entire range of library resources regardless of content, approach, format, or amount of detail. This principle of library service applies equally to all users, minors as well as adults. Librarians and library governing bodies must uphold this principle in order to provide adequate and effective service to minors.

Policies that set minimum age limits for access to any nonprint materials or information technology, with or without parental permission, abridge library use for minors. Age limits based on the cost of the materials are also unacceptable. Librarians, when dealing with minors, should apply the same standards to circulation of nonprint materials as are applied to books and other print materials except when directly and specifically prohibited by law.

Recognizing that librarians cannot act *in loco parentis,* ALA acknowledges and supports the exercise by parents of their responsibility to guide their own children's reading and viewing. Libraries should provide published reviews and/or reference works that contain information about the content, subject matter, and recommended audiences for nonprint materials. These resources will assist parents in guiding their children without implicating the library in censorship.

In some cases, commercial content ratings, such as the Motion Picture Association of America (MPAA) movie ratings, might appear on the packaging or promotional materials provided by producers or distributors. However, marking out or removing this information from materials or packaging constitutes expurgation or censorship.

MPAA movie ratings, Entertainment Software Rating Board (ESRB) game ratings, and other rating services are private advisory codes and have no legal standing ("Expurgation of Library Materials"). For the library to add ratings to nonprint materials if they are not already there is unacceptable. It is also unacceptable to post a list of such ratings with a collection or to use them in circulation policies or other procedures. These uses constitute labeling, "an attempt to prejudice attitudes" ("Labeling and Rating Systems"), and are forms of censorship. The application of locally generated ratings schemes intended to provide content warnings to library users is also inconsistent with the Library Bill of Rights.

The interests of young people, like those of adults, are not limited by subject, theme, or level of sophistication. Librarians have a responsibility to ensure young people's access to materials and services that reflect diversity of content and format sufficient to meet their needs.

Adopted June 28, 1989, by the ALA Council; amended June 30, 2004.

ACCESS TO RESOURCES AND SERVICES IN THE SCHOOL LIBRARY MEDIA PROGRAM

An Interpretation of the Library Bill of Rights

THE SCHOOL library media program plays a unique role in promoting intellectual freedom. It serves as a point of voluntary access to information and ideas and as a learning laboratory for students as they acquire critical thinking and problem-solving skills needed in a pluralistic society. Although the educational level and program of the school necessarily shape the resources and services of a school library media program, the principles of the Library Bill of Rights apply equally to all libraries, including school library media programs. Under these principles, all students have equitable access to library facilities, resources, and instructional programs.

School library media specialists assume a leadership role in promoting the principles of intellectual freedom within the school by providing resources and services that create and sustain an atmosphere of free inquiry. School library media specialists work closely with teachers to integrate instructional activities in classroom units designed to equip students to locate, evaluate, and use a broad range of ideas effectively. Intellectual freedom is fostered by educating students in the use of critical thinking skills to empower them to pursue free inquiry responsibly and independently. Through resources, programming, and educational processes, students and teachers experience the free and robust debate characteristic of a democratic society.

School library media specialists cooperate with other individuals in building collections of resources that meet the needs as well as the developmental and maturity levels of students. These collections provide resources that support the mission of the school district and are consistent with its philosophy, goals, and objectives. Resources in school library media collections are an integral component of the curriculum and represent diverse points of view on both current and historical issues. These resources include materials that support the intellectual growth, personal development, individual interests, and recreational needs of students.

While English is, by history and tradition, the customary language of the United States, the languages in use in any given community may vary. Schools serving communities in which other languages are used make efforts to accommodate the needs of students for whom English is a second language. To support these efforts, and to ensure equitable access to resources and services, the school library media program provides resources that reflect the linguistic pluralism of the community.

Members of the school community involved in the collection development process employ educational criteria to select resources unfettered by their personal, political, social, or religious views. Students and educators served by the school library media program have access to resources and services free of constraints resulting from personal, partisan, or doctrinal disapproval. School library media specialists resist efforts by individuals or groups to define what is appropriate for all students or teachers to read, view, hear, or access via electronic means.

Major barriers between students and resources include but are not limited to imposing age, grade-level, or reading-level restrictions on the use of resources; limiting the use of interlibrary loan and access to electronic information; charging fees for information in specific formats; requiring permission from parents or teachers; establishing restricted shelves or closed collections; and labeling. Policies, procedures, and rules related to the use of resources and services support free and open access to information.

It is the responsibility of the governing board to adopt policies that guarantee students access to a broad range of ideas. These include policies on collection development and procedures for the review of resources about which concerns have been raised. Such policies, developed by persons in the school community, provide for a timely and fair hearing and assure that procedures are applied equitably to all expressions of concern. It is the responsibility of school library media specialists to implement district policies and procedures in the school to ensure equitable access to resources and services for all students.

Adopted July 2, 1986, by the ALA Council; amended January 10, 1990; July 12, 2000; January 19, 2005; July 2, 2008.

MINORS AND INTERNET INTERACTIVITY

An Interpretation of the Library Bill of Rights

THE DIGITAL environment offers opportunities for accessing, creating, and sharing information. The rights of minors to retrieve, interact with, and create information posted on the Internet in schools and libraries are extensions of their First Amendment rights. (See also other interpretations of the Library Bill of Rights, including "Access to Digital Information, Services, and Networks," "Free Access to Libraries for Minors," and "Access for Children and Young Adults to Nonprint Materials.")

Academic pursuits of minors can be strengthened with the use of interactive Web tools, allowing young people to create documents and share them online; upload pictures, videos, and graphic material; revise public documents; and add tags to online content to classify and organize information. Instances of inappropriate use of such academic tools should be addressed as individual behavior issues, not as justification for restricting or banning access to interactive technology. Schools and libraries should ensure that institutional environments offer opportunities for students to use interactive Web tools constructively in their academic pursuits, as the benefits of shared learning are well documented.

Personal interactions of minors can be enhanced by social tools available through the Internet. Social networking websites allow the creation of online communities that feature an open exchange of information in various forms, such as images, videos, blog posts, and discussions about common interests. Interactive Web tools help children and young adults learn about and organize social, civic, and extracurricular activities. Many interactive sites invite users to establish online identities, share personal information, create Web content, and join social networks. Parents and guardians play a critical role in preparing their children for participation in online activity by communicating their personal family values and by monitoring their children's use of the Internet. Parents and guardians are responsible for what their children—and only their children—access on the Internet in libraries.

The use of interactive Web tools poses two competing intellectual freedom issues—the protection of minors' privacy and the right of free speech. Some have expressed concerns regarding what they perceive is an increased vulnerability of young people in the online environment when they use interactive sites to post personally identifiable information. In an effort to protect minors' privacy, adults sometimes restrict access to interactive Web environments. Filters, for example, are sometimes used to restrict access by youth to interactive social networking tools, but at the same time deny minors' rights to free expression on the Internet. Prohibiting children and young adults from using social networking sites does not teach safe behavior and leaves youth without the necessary knowledge and skills to protect their privacy or engage in responsible speech. Instead of restricting or denying access to the Internet, librarians and teachers should educate minors to participate responsibly, ethically, and safely.

The First Amendment applies to speech created by minors on interactive sites. Usage of these social networking sites in a school or library allows minors to access and create resources that fulfill their interests and needs for information, for social connection with peers, and for participation in a community of learners. Restricting expression and access to interactive websites because the sites provide tools for sharing information with others violates the tenets of the Library Bill of Rights. It is the responsibility of librarians and educators to monitor threats to the intellectual freedom of minors and to advocate for extending access to interactive applications on the Internet.

As defenders of intellectual freedom and the First Amendment, libraries and librarians have a responsibility to offer unrestricted access to Internet interactivity in accordance with local, state, and federal laws and to advocate for greater access where it is abridged. School and library professionals should work closely with young people to help them learn skills and attitudes that will prepare them to be responsible, effective, and productive communicators in a free society.

Adopted July 15, 2009, by the ALA Council.

LABELING AND RATING SYSTEMS

An Interpretation of the Library Bill of Rights

LIBRARIES DO not advocate the ideas found in their collections or in resources accessible through the library. The presence of books and other resources in a library does not indicate endorsement of their contents by the library. Likewise, providing access to digital information does not indicate endorsement or approval of that information by the library. Labeling and rating systems present distinct challenges to these intellectual freedom principles.

Labels on library materials may be viewpoint-neutral directional aids designed to save the time of users, or they may be attempts to prejudice or discourage users or restrict their access to materials. When labeling is an attempt to prejudice attitudes, it is a censor's tool. The American Library Association opposes labeling as a means of predisposing people's attitudes toward library materials.

Prejudicial labels are designed to restrict access, based on a value judgment that the content, language, or themes of the material, or the background or views of the creator(s) of the material, render it inappropriate or offensive for all or certain groups of users. The prejudicial label is used to warn, discourage, or prohibit users or certain groups of users from accessing the material. Such labels sometimes are used to place materials in restricted locations where access depends on staff intervention.

Viewpoint-neutral directional aids facilitate access by making it easier for users to locate materials. The materials are housed on open shelves and are equally accessible to all users, who may choose to consult or ignore the directional aids at their own discretion.

Directional aids can have the effect of prejudicial labels when their implementation becomes proscriptive rather than descriptive. When directional aids are used to forbid access or to suggest moral or doctrinal endorsement, the effect is the same as prejudicial labeling.

Many organizations use rating systems as a means of advising either their members or the general public regarding the organizations' opinions of the contents and suitability or appropriate age for use of certain books, films, recordings, websites, games, or other materials. The adoption, enforcement, or endorsement of any of these rating systems by a library violates the Library Bill of Rights. When requested, librarians should provide information about rating systems equitably, regardless of viewpoint.

Adopting such systems into law or library policy may be unconstitutional. If labeling or rating systems are mandated by law, the library should seek legal advice regarding the law's applicability to library operations.

Libraries sometimes acquire resources that include ratings as part of their packaging. Librarians should not endorse the inclusion of such rating systems; however, removing or destroying the ratings—if placed there by, or with permission of, the copyright holder—could constitute expurgation. (See "Expurgation of Library Materials: An Interpretation of the Library Bill of Rights.") In addition, the inclusion of ratings on bibliographic records in library catalogs is a violation of the Library Bill of Rights.

Prejudicial labeling and ratings presuppose the existence of individuals or groups with wisdom to determine by authority what is appropriate or inappropriate for others. They presuppose that individuals must be directed in making up their minds about the ideas they examine. The American Library Association affirms the rights of individuals to form their own opinions about resources they choose to read or view.

Adopted July 13, 1951, by the ALA Council; amended June 25, 1971; July 1, 1981; June 26, 1990; January 19, 2005; July 15, 2009.

QUESTIONS AND ANSWERS ON LABELS AND RATING SYSTEMS

Preamble

Librarians employ objective professional judgment through selection, cataloging, classification, and readers' services to make available the information that library users want or need. Cataloging decisions, labels, or ratings applied in an attempt to restrict or discourage access to materials or to suggest moral or doctrinal endorsement is a violation of the First Amendment and the Library Bill of Rights. [See "Labeling and Rating Systems: An Interpretation of the Library Bill of Rights."]

Definitions

What is the difference between a viewpoint-neutral directional aid and a prejudicial label?

Labels and rating systems produced by libraries, publishers, and organizations can be valuable and convenient aids for assisting library users and staff in finding and selecting desired materials.

These tools are not de facto viewpoint-neutral directional aids or prejudicial labels; they become so only according to their implementation.

Any existing or proposed rating systems should be examined in light of intellectual freedom principles.

Genres

What are examples for determining whether a genre label is a viewpoint-neutral directional aid or a prejudicial label?

Fiction genre labels such as romance, mystery, and science fiction are used by many libraries as viewpoint-neutral direction aids. While there may be some differences of opinion about which titles fit within specific genre areas, the choice of genre is viewpoint neutral and does not suggest moral or doctrinal endorsement.

On the other hand, some public libraries label Christian fiction with a cross as a symbol. This practice, especially when other religious fiction is not designated, communicates a message of preference for Christianity, a violation of the separation of church and state that is prohibited by the establishment clause of the First Amendment as well as the Library Bill of Rights.

People of all persuasions and traditions have sincere, heartfelt concerns when their government addresses religious issues, fundamentally different from an interest as to whether a library item bears a "Mystery" or "Western" sticker. In recognition of this, some libraries seek to avoid entanglement with religion by using a label to identify "inspirational fiction," including material that does not have religious-based content. As long as both the selection of materials to be so labeled and the label used are viewpoint neutral and inclusive, this practice would not violate the Library Bill of Rights.

Enhanced Content in Catalogs

Does the practice of bundling bibliographic records with databases and other electronic informational resources including book reviews, book covers, and other evaluative materials violate the Library Bill of Rights?

Some vendors provide bibliographic records enhanced with databases and other electronic informational resources including book reviews and other evaluative materials.

The interpretation on "Labeling and Rating Systems" should not be construed to preclude provision of resources and information useful to users as they make their choices from the library's catalog as long as the criteria for inclusion is viewpoint neutral.

Libraries should seek the broadest spectrum of informational and evaluative materials as possible. Furthermore, the library profession should advocate to vendors for the inclusion of diverse viewpoints in the products they develop for libraries.

Is it appropriate to add movie, game, or music ratings to the bibliographic record?

No. These rating systems are devised by private groups using subjective and changing criteria to advise people of suitability or content of materials. It is the library's responsibility to prevent the imposition or endorsement of private rating systems. Including such ratings in the bibliographic record, library records, and other library authored finding aids would predispose people's attitudes toward the material and thus violate the Library Bill of Rights.

Rating Systems and the Library

What if a group develops a rating system? What would ALA advise?

Any private group's rating system, regardless of political, doctrinal, or social viewpoint, is subjective and meant to predispose the public's attitude, and therefore violates the Library Bill of Rights. Libraries should remain viewpoint neutral, providing information users seek about any rating system equitably, regardless of the group's viewpoint.

What if a library board is asked to use movie, video game, music, or other ratings to restrict access?

A variety of private organizations including the Classification and Rating Administration (CARA) of the Motion Picture Association of America (MPAA), Canadian Motion Picture Distributors Association, PSVratings Standards Board (PSV), Parents Television Council (PTC), Entertainment Software Rating Board (ESRB), TV Parental Guidelines Monitoring Board, and the Recording Industry Association of America (RIAA) have developed rating systems as a means of advising parents concerning their opinions of the contents and suitability or appropriate age for use of certain books, films, recordings, television programs, websites, or other materials.

None of these organizations are government agencies and as such their rating systems cannot be mandated or enforced by any government or agency of government, including a publicly funded library. A library can, however, make information concerning these rating systems available to library users.

For more information on this topic see Deborah Caldwell-Stone, "Movie Ratings are Private, Not Public Policy," *Illinois Library Association Reporter* 22:2 (2004): 10–13.

Is it prejudicial to describe violent and sexual content? For example, would including "contains mild violence" on bibliographic record of a graphic novel violate the Library Bill of Rights?

Yes. In any community there will be a range of attitudes as to what is deemed offensive and contrary to moral values. For some the issue is sexually explicit content, for others the concern is with violence, for still others it is language. Including notes in the bibliographic record regarding what may be objectionable content assumes all members of the community hold the same values. No one person should take responsibility for judging what is offensive. Such voluntary labeling in bibliographic records and catalogs violates the Library Bill of Rights.

Age, Grade, Reading Level, and Computerized Reading Programs

I would like to organize sections of the library using reading level designations, such as those supplied by Accelerated Reader. Is this okay?

While knowing the reading level of a book can assist library users, organizing a library via these labels can pose a psychological barrier for users who do not know their reading level. Many will feel that they should not utilize those resources.

Users who do know their reading level may feel compelled to only select resources from their reading level. This will result in users not utilizing the full scope of the library collection.

Is it okay to restrict certain sections of the collection based on the patron's age or grade level?

Restricting access to library materials based on age or grade level does not respect the individual needs, interests, and abilities of users and violates the Library Bill of Rights.

All students in my school are required to participate in a computerized reading program that assigns reading levels and point values to books and tests students for reading comprehension. Parents and teachers want library books placed on the shelves by reading level so that students can easily access and be limited to books that meet their individual needs. This would be easy to do since the vendor sells preprinted labels for grade level and point value designation. Is this acceptable?

No. A student should have access to all materials in a school library.

The chronological age or grade level of students is not representative of their information needs or total reading abilities. If collections are organized by age or grade, some users will feel inhibited from selecting resources from sections that do not correspond to their exact characteristics. If the library limits users from checking out resources from sections other than those that match the patron's characteristics, the library will most likely not serve the needs of users.

While some parents and teachers may find housing books by grade level helpful in guiding developing young readers, a library should not use such labels as a classification system, or to promote any restrictive or prejudicial practice. Most computerized reading programs list books by grade levels on their websites if parents and teachers wish to seek such direction.

My library users participate in the Accelerated Reader program, and we feel pressured to purchase books that are on the reading lists. Some of the books on these lists are recommended for reading levels that match the abilities of my users, but I question the emotional and maturity levels of the themes of the books. What do I do?

While lists from programs like Accelerated Reader may be helpful in selecting books for a school or public library in school districts where such programs are a prominent part of the curriculum, it is important to remember that emotional and maturity levels do not necessarily correlate with reading level. A library or school district should have a selection policy that specifically outlines how materials are selected and what resources are used. This may include specific review journals and other professional collection development tools. Librarians should advise teachers and administrators that their responsibility is to practice good selection, and to follow the selection policy of the institution. This may mean that some books on the Accelerated Reader lists that are recommended for high-achieving young readers may not be selected because of the maturity level.

Recommended Book Lists

A local school has a required summer reading list. Our library pulls them from the general collection and places them together. Is that considered viewpoint neutral?

Yes. Assembling materials that will be in high demand for a limited period of time helps library users find them. Such selections should be accessible to all users and not limited to the target audience.

Labeling Based on Ethnic or Language Group

We have a large population of a specific ethnic/language group in our service area and we would like to create a section of the library and a collection to recognize that. Is that acceptable and how may we go about it?

When there is a large population of a specific ethnic or language group in an area, it often creates a large demand for items relevant to their experience in the library. To meet that demand and make it simpler for the users to locate those resources, libraries sometimes choose to create a special collection and/or area devoted to those resources. As long as these collections represent diverse points of view within the parameters of the collection and are designed to help patrons find resources relevant to their experience and not to restrict them to a certain section of the library, this practice would be acceptable.

American Library Association
April 6, 2006

CODE OF ETHICS OF THE AMERICAN LIBRARY ASSOCIATION

AS MEMBERS of the American Library Association, we recognize the importance of codifying and making known to the profession and to the general public the ethical principles that guide the work of librarians, other professionals providing information services, library trustees, and library staffs.

Ethical dilemmas occur when values are in conflict. The American Library Association Code of Ethics states the values to which we are committed, and embodies the ethical responsibilities of the profession in this changing information environment.

We significantly influence or control the selection, organization, preservation, and dissemination of information. In a political system grounded in an informed citizenry, we are members of a profession explicitly committed to intellectual freedom and the freedom of access to information. We have a special obligation to ensure the free flow of information and ideas to present and future generations.

The principles of this Code are expressed in broad statements to guide ethical decision making. These statements provide a framework; they cannot and do not dictate conduct to cover particular situations.

> I. We provide the highest level of service to all library users through appropriate and usefully organized resources; equitable service

policies; equitable access; and accurate, unbiased, and courteous responses to all requests.

II. We uphold the principles of intellectual freedom and resist all efforts to censor library resources.

III. We protect each library user's right to privacy and confidentiality with respect to information sought or received and resources consulted, borrowed, acquired, or transmitted.

IV. We respect intellectual property rights and advocate balance between the interests of information users and rights holders.

V. We treat coworkers and other colleagues with respect, fairness, and good faith, and advocate conditions of employment that safeguard the rights and welfare of all employees of our institutions.

VI. We do not advance private interests at the expense of library users, colleagues, or our employing institutions.

VII. We distinguish between our personal convictions and professional duties and do not allow our personal beliefs to interfere with fair representation of the aims of our institutions or the provision of access to their information resources.

VIII. We strive for excellence in the profession by maintaining and enhancing our own knowledge and skills, by encouraging the professional development of coworkers, and by fostering the aspirations of potential members of the profession.

Adopted January 22, 2008, by the ALA Council.

GUIDELINES FOR LIBRARY SERVICES TO TEENS, AGES 12-18

By YALSA and RUSA

Foreword

These guidelines were created in 2006 by a joint task force of members of both the Reference and User Services Association (RUSA) and the Young Adult Library Services Association (YALSA). Members of the task force were Sarah Flowers, Helen Hejny, Rosemary Chance, Mary K. Chelton, David Fuller, and Stephen Matthews.

Introduction

Teens are substantial users of public libraries (NCES, 1995) and the primary users of secondary school libraries. Their presence and numbers, as well as their developmental characteristics and life circumstances, present a distinct challenge for reference service providers. During adolescence, teens develop the ability to hypothesize and think about the future and foresee consequences for actions. They also develop personal ethics and critical thinking abilities. At the same time, they are extremely self-conscious, which makes them easily embarrassed. All of these factors combine to make reference service to teens unique and uniquely challenging. It is our hope that these guidelines will help reference librarians in all kinds of libraries provide excellent service to teens.

Guidelines

1.0 Integrate library service to teens into the overall library plan, budget, and service program.

It is essential for the leaders and policy makers of the library to understand that service for teens is not a fad; that the need and demand for library services will only increase; that teens have specific library service needs that are different from those of children or adults; and that nothing short of a total moral and financial commitment to library services for teens will meet the needs and demands of the present and future teen library user.

1.1 Acknowledge the educational and developmental needs of teens in the library's strategic planning and evaluation process.
1.2 Incorporate funding for materials and services for teens in the library's operating budget.
1.3 Actively seek supplemental funding for programs and services to teens.
1.4 Provide spaces and collections for teens that are separate from children's spaces and collections.

2.0 Provide teens with courteous and professional customer service at every service point.

Friendly, positive, and unbiased customer interactions are the goal of every public service provider. This is especially true in the world of libraries, as we strive to offer courteous professional services to all library users. All library customers, regardless of age, benefit when library staff fosters a knowledgeable, friendly, and inviting atmosphere.

2.1 Promote a more beneficial working relationship with teens through continuous staff development and education.
2.2 Integrate library services to teens with those offered to other user populations.
2.3 Assure that services for teens embrace cultural diversity and economic differences.
2.4 Train all staff members to respect the teen's need for privacy and nonjudgmental service.

2.5 Provide services by teen specialists or certified school library media specialists as well as by others who are trained to serve teens.

3.0   Use the most current information and communication technologies, the connections that they use on a daily basis, to provide information to teens.

Online information and electronic communication is a way of life for most teens. They have come of age with the Web, the iPod, cable and satellite television, the cell phone, etc., and these tools form a seamless part of their everyday lives. Change and innovation are and will be the defining forces in personal technology so this list of gadgets and interfaces will expand and change as the "ways to be wired" morph and grow. Librarians need to understand how these "digital natives" perceive the world. We need to provide direction, structure, and effective assistance, both when we are asked directly to help as well as when we are not. Sound and savvy instruction in information literacy and thoughtful design of intuitive and welcoming portals to our virtual libraries are essential allies in serving the needs of teens.

3.1 Provide unfettered and convenient access to licensed databases and other online library resources for teens.

3.2 Incorporate the use of social networking (e.g., instant messaging, blogs, and social websites) into service plans that are designed to provide reference services to teens.

3.3 Employ in-person as well as digital (online tutorials, help screens, search process prompts) methods of information literacy instruction at the point of service.

3.4 Develop and promote homework assistance websites/portals as key elements in meeting the information needs of teens.

3.5 Ensure that teens receive the same high quality of online reference service as all other users.

3.6 Endeavor to make online reference services available 24/7 to accommodate teens' busy lifestyles and often unpredictable study and research habits.

4.0   Provide and promote information and resources appropriate to both curriculum and leisure needs of teens.

Teens approach the reference desk with two main types of questions: the "imposed" query (usually a school assignment) and the personal query (often a popular culture interest). Maintaining a collection that is relevant to the interests and needs of teens will help to maintain the relevance of the library in their lives. The library's role extends beyond gathering resources to keeping them current and actively seeking means to publicize and promote them. The library should be positioned as a primary access point to information on everything from school curriculum topics to college planning, health issues, career opportunities, and popular culture.

4.1 Develop collections to reflect the information needs and interests of teens.

4.2 Take the requests of teens seriously, and ask for their input in developing collections for them.

4.3 Recognize that homework is a major part of teen information-seeking and that homework assistance is a necessary service for this age group.

4.4 Recognize that teens often do not know or are not interested in the content of what they are asking, but only know that they have to have it, usually at once.

4.5 Provide a variety of formats for information and resources, such as audiobooks, databases, Internet access, and listening equipment, as well as computer programs such as word processing, spreadsheet, database, and Web publishing software for homework assignments, class projects, and recreational use.

5.0   Provide library services and programs appropriate for teens.

Libraries should provide a community setting for teen programming that will ultimately enable teens to develop new library skills, to become independent and skillful library users, and to enjoy traditional informational or recreational programs.

5.1 Provide positive programming to meet the needs and interests of teens and their family members as well as opportunities for teens to experience ownership of the library by contributing collection suggestions and situations in which they can share their expertise (with reading, technology, hobbies, etc.).

5.2 Create activities that promote growth and development such as community service hours, volunteer opportunities, and projects that help develop a sense of responsibility.

5.3 Guide teens to become self-sufficient library users through example and pertinent activities and positive programs specifically designed to meet their interests.

5.4 Develop programming and services to meet the needs of teens unable to visit the library through technology and outreach.

5.5 Publicize services and programs for teens in popular local establishments and using current technology trends.

5.6 Actively involve teens in planning and implementing services and programs for their age group through advisory boards, task forces, and by less formal means (i.e., surveys, one-on-one discussion, focus groups, etc.).

6.0 Cultivate partnerships with community agencies and groups serving teens.

Library programs and services for teens should not replicate those of other agencies, but can complement and support them. Investigate possible joint programs for teens. Identify resources the library can provide to assist professionals who work with teens.

6.1 Identify community organizations and groups of and for teens.

6.2 Collaborate with schools in areas such as class assignments, reading lists, and bibliographic instruction to more effectively serve teens with their academic needs.

6.3 Collaborate with other organizations serving teens such as youth groups and after-school programs.

6.4 Partner with schools and local organizations for library programs and delivery of services.

RESOURCES

Alexander, Jonathan. *Digital Youth: Emerging Literacies on the World Wide Web.* Cresskill, NJ: Hampton Press, 2006.

Bolan, Kimberly, Meg Canada, and Rob Cullin. "Web, Library, and Teen Services 2.0." *Young Adult Library Services* 5, no. 2:40–43.

Chelton, Mary K. "Perspectives on YA Practice—Common YA Models of Service in Public Libraries—Advantages and Disadvantages." *Young Adult Library Services* 3, no. 4:4–6, 11.

Chelton, Mary K., and Colleen Cool, eds. *Youth Information-Seeking Behavior: Theories, Models, and Issues.* Lanham, MD: Scarecrow Press, 2004.

Chelton, Mary K., and Colleen Cool, eds. *Youth Information-Seeking Behavior II: Context, Theories, Models, and Issues.* Lanham, MD: Scarecrow Press, 2007.

Farmer, Lesley S. J. *Digital Inclusion, Teens, and Your Library.* Westport, CT: Libraries Unlimited, 2005.

Gross, Melissa. "Imposed Query." *RQ* 35, no. 1:236–43.

Harris, Frances Jacobson. *I Found It on the Internet: Coming of Age Online.* Chicago: American Library Association, 2005.

Honnold, RoseMary. *101+ Teen Programs That Work.* New York: Neal-Schuman Publishers, 2003.

Jones, Patrick, and Joe Shoemaker. *Do It Right! Best Practices for Serving Young Adults in School and Public Libraries.* New York: Neal-Schuman Publishers, 2001.

Jones, Patrick, Michele Gorman, and Tricia Suellentrop. *Connecting Young Adults and Libraries: A How-To-Do-It Manual for Librarians,* 3rd ed. New York: Neal-Schuman Publishers, 2004.

Knowles, Elizabeth, and Martha Smith. *Reading Rules! Motivating Teens to Read.* Westport, CT: Libraries Unlimited, 2001.

Mahood, Kristine. *A Passion for Print: Promoting Reading and Books to Teens.* Westport, CT: Libraries Unlimited, 2006.

Vaillancourt, Renee J. *Managing Young Adult Services: A Self-Help Manual.* New York: Neal-Schuman Publishers, 2002.

YALSA. "Young Adults Deserve the Best: Competencies for Librarians Serving Youth." www.ala.org/yalsa/competencies/.

YALSA, with Patrick Jones. *New Directions for Library Service to Young Adults.* Chicago: American Library Association, 2002.

REFERENCES

Chelton, Mary K., "Adult-Adolescent Service Encounters: The Library Context" (doctoral dissertation, Rutgers University, 1997).

National Center for Education Statistics, *Services for Children and Young Adults in Public Libraries* (NCES 95-731) (Washington, DC: U.S. Government Printing Office, 1995).

INDEX

You may also be interested in

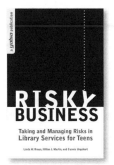

Risky Business: Real-world examples of risky change in action from librarians and authors of YA lit enrich this exploration of a topic rarely discussed in depth, but central to YA services in school and public libraries today.

Multicultural Programs for Tweens and Teens: A one-stop resource that encourages children and young adults to explore different cultures, this book includes programs specific to your scheduling, budget, or age group requirements, event ideas that reflect specific cultures, recommend further resources, and much more.

Quick and Popular Reads for Teens: This reference source compiles bibliographic information about the books honored by YALSA's two annual lists: *Popular Paperbacks for Young Adults* and *Quick Picks for Reluctant Readers*, which consist of recommended reading targeted at young adults who are not avid readers.

A Year of Programs for Teens 2: In this sequel to the book that "takes teen services to a new level" (*Adolescence*), YA experts Amy J. Alessio and Kimberly A. Patton present entirely fresh content with several new themed book lists and read-alikes as well as appendixes with reproducible handouts for the various programs.

Order today at www.alastore.ala.org or 866-746-7252!